table of contents

acknowledgments

4

I must confess that when we decided to create this cookbook, I thought it could be done very easily. Wrong! Without the help of some very dedicated people, this would have been an impossible task. So, I want to thank the wonderful supporters who helped to make it all happen.

My deepest thanks go to:

My soulmate and wife, Rosa, for her encouragement and hard work troubleshooting, recreating and testing all of the recipes.

My sons, Andrew and Daniel, for eating everything I make with such gusto. Special thanks to Andrew for the wonderful photographs that appear throughout the book and on the cover.

My business partner, Paolo Paolini, for generously giving me the time to invest in this book and for wearing his heart on his sleeve.

The staff at Mistura and Sopra for looking after the restaurants (and me) so well. Special thanks to Peter Sananagan for running around gathering ingredients for the photography.

Marilyn Denis and the producers of "Cityline with Marilyn Denis" for inviting me to be on the show. My constant search for simple recipes to share with viewers resulted in this book.

ONE POT ITALIAN COOKING

MASSIMO CAPRA

Photographs By Christopher Campbell

A Madison Press Book

Text, cover, design and compilation © 2007 The Madison Press Limited
Recipe text © Massimo Capra
Photographs © Christopher Campbell, www.christophercampbell.net,
except as credited on page 192

First published in the United Kingdom in 2007

A catalogue record for this book is available from the British Library

ISBN-13: 978-1-897330-25-8
ISBN-10: 1-897330-25-1

1 3 5 7 9 10 8 6 4 2

Produced by
Madison Press Books
1000 Yonge Street, Suite 200
Toronto, Ontario
M4W 2K2
madisonpressbooks.com

Printed in Singapore
by Imago Productions (F.E.) Ltd., Singapore

The producers and crew of "Restaurant Makeover" for giving me fresh perspective and keeping me inspired with new ideas for my craft.

The freelance professionals and staff at Madison for guiding me to make the best book possible: Christopher Campbell and Dennis Wood for beautiful food photographs; Judy Phillips for smooth sentences; Kerry Plumley and Diana Sullada for tasteful art direction; Alison Maclean for clearing up my anxiety and keeping me on track; and special thanks to Al Cummings for believing in me and being there whenever I need him.

The patrons of my restaurants for understanding the beauty and simplicity of honest food, and for your constant support.

And my parents, who have my loving thanks and to whom I dedicate this book.

Un abbraccio a tuttti,

Massimo Capra
June 1, 2007

zuppe e minestre / soups

ribollita
tuscan cabbage soup

Ribollita is one of the most popular Tuscan soups. I turn to it whenever I'm in need of some soul food. This is a great soup to make ahead of time, as it can be frozen and reheated later without compromising the flavor.

Note: Soak the navy beans overnight in cold water. Rinse well under cold running water before using. Alternatively, do a quick soak by bringing the beans to a boil, turning off the heat, and letting stand for 1 hour.

Makes 8 servings

2 tbsp/30 mL extra-virgin olive oil	2 large tomatoes, chopped
4 cloves garlic, finely chopped	2 tsp/10 mL chopped fresh thyme or $\frac{1}{2}$ tsp/2 mL dried thyme
4 bay leaves	
1 large onion, finely chopped	$\frac{1}{4}$ tsp/2 mL salt
2 large carrots, peeled and diced	$\frac{1}{2}$ tsp/1 mL freshly ground black pepper
1 stalk celery, diced	
8 cups/2 L vegetable stock or water	$\frac{1}{2}$ loaf Italian bread, cut into $\frac{1}{2}$-inch (1 cm) slices (about 16 slices)
1 cup/250 mL dried navy beans, presoaked	$\frac{1}{2}$ cup/160 mL freshly grated Parmesan cheese
3 cups/750 mL shredded cabbage	

Heat the olive oil in a large saucepan over medium heat. Sauté the garlic and bay leaves for 3 minutes. Add the onion, carrot, and celery, and cook for 4 minutes, or until softened. Add the beans and the vegetable stock or water and bring to a boil. Reduce the heat and simmer for 40 minutes, or until the beans are tender. Stir in the cabbage, tomatoes, thyme, salt, and pepper. Simmer for 5 minutes, then remove the bay leaves.

In the meantime, preheat the oven to 350°F (180°C). Toast the bread slices for 15 minutes, or until lightly browned.

Pour a third of the bean mixture into a 13x9-inch (3 L) baking dish. Top with half of the bread slices. Repeat the layers, ending with the bean mixture and making sure all the bread is moistened. Sprinkle with Parmesan. Bake for 45 minutes, or until the top is bubbling and golden brown.

risi e bisi
rice and pea soup

This soup is a springtime favorite in Italy's Veneto region. Many people know this dish as a risotto, but it is really more of a thick soup. The tender, sweet peas are delicious to bite into, and the chicken broth offers an extra layer of flavor that will keep you coming back for more.

Makes 4 servings

2 tbsp/30 mL butter

2 tbsp/30 mL chopped onion

6 oz/170 g pancetta, chopped

12 oz/340 g shelled fresh green peas

8 cups/2 L chicken stock

3½ cups/875 mL vialone nano or other risotto rice

½ cup/125 mL chopped Italian parsley

salt and pepper

1 cup/250 mL grated grana padano cheese

Melt 1 tbsp/15 mL of the butter in a large skillet over medium heat. Add the onion and pancetta and sauté until soft. Stir in the peas and cook for about 1 minute, then add the chicken stock and bring to a boil.

Add the rice and parsley and simmer until the rice is cooked but still firm to the bite, about 14–17 minutes. The mixture should look dense, but with more liquid than a risotto. Season to taste with salt and pepper.

Remove from heat and gently stir in the remaining 1 tbsp/15 mL butter and the grana padano. Serve at once. ☞

pappa al pomodoro
tuscan tomato soup

If you think that making soup is difficult, this recipe will change your mind. The key to this soup is the quality of the tomatoes. This recipe calls for canned tomatoes—buy the best quality possible. But use fresh, ripe red tomatoes when they're in season, or experiment by using yellow or orange tomatoes.

Makes 4–6 servings

4 tbsp/60 mL extra-virgin olive oil	salt and pepper
1 large onion, finely chopped	2 cups/500 mL diced country-style white bread, preferably stale
4 cloves garlic, crushed	1 bunch basil, chopped
3 cups/750 mL canned plum (Roma) tomatoes, seeds removed	grated Parmigiano-Reggiano or pecorino cheese, for garnish
2 cups/500 mL vegetable stock	extra-virgin olive oil, for garnish

Heat the olive oil in a stockpot over medium heat. Add the onion and garlic; sauté until the onion is translucent. Add the tomatoes and cook for 3–4 minutes to blend the flavors. Pour in the stock and simmer for 15 minutes.

Season to taste with salt and pepper. Stir in the bread and basil, and cook until the bread has a creamy consistency.

Serve with a generous sprinkle of grated Parmigiano-Reggiano or pecorino and a drizzle of extra-virgin olive oil.

Variation 1

Substitute 1 cup/250 mL of heavy cream for the bread, and blend the soup until smooth before adding the basil. This version is a favorite with kids.

Variation 2

For a clear, light tomato soup, use rice or pasta instead of bread.

Variation 3

For a great minestrone, just add chopped vegetables of your choice and simmer until they are cooked through. 🥘

zuppa di castagne
chestnut soup

This unusual but elegant soup is a good choice for a special dinner when you want to impress your guests, but it also makes a satisfyingly rib-sticking, eat-beside-the-fire kind of soup—terrific with garlic toast. Chestnuts are simple to roast, but if you prefer, buy vacuum-packed chestnuts that have already been roasted.

Note: To roast the chestnuts, soak them first in water for 2 hours. Score and roast in a 500°F (260°C) oven for 7–10 minutes. Once they are cool enough to touch, shell them—the shell and brown skin should come off easily.

Makes 4–6 servings

2 tbsp/30 mL extra-virgin olive oil	2 bay leaves
½ cup/125 mL diced pancetta	4 cups/1 L chicken stock
2 cloves garlic, crushed	extra-virgin olive oil and Parmigiano-Reggiano cheese, for garnish
1 cup/250 mL finely diced onion	
½ cup/125 mL finely diced celery	OR
½ cup/125 mL finely diced carrot	sour cream and chopped chives, for garnish
4 cups/1 L roasted chestnuts, skinned	

Heat the olive oil in a large stockpot over medium heat. Add the pancetta, garlic, onion, celery, and carrots, and sauté until the vegetables are translucent. Add 3 cups/750 mL of the roasted chestnuts along with the bay leaves and chicken stock, and simmer for 15 minutes.

Remove the soup from the heat, discard the bay leaves, and puree in a blender. Strain to refine the soup and remove any hard pieces of chestnut.

Return the strained soup to the heat, add the remaining 1 cup/250 mL of chestnuts, and simmer for another 5 minutes.

Serve with a sprinkle of extra-virgin olive oil and grated Parmigiano-Reggiano, or with a dollop of sour cream and chopped chives.

minestrone di massimo
massimo's fall harvest vegetable soup

Every cook has his or her own style of minestrone. Here's mine, with lots of soft, colorful, and sweet autumn vegetables. The only rule that applies to this soup is the way the vegetables are cut—it will influence the soup's look and the way it feels to the palate. Cut the vegetables quite small so that there is a variety in every spoonful. This recipe calls for six cloves of garlic, but feel free to add even more if you like.

Makes 6–8 servings

6 cloves garlic, crushed

4 tbsp/60 mL olive oil

1 cup/250 mL minced onion

1 cup/250 mL sliced celery hearts (tender innermost stalks)

1 cup/250 mL sliced carrot

1 cup/250 mL seeded and diced green and yellow zucchini

1 sprig fresh thyme

4 bay leaves

6 cups/1.5 L vegetable stock

salt and pepper

1 cup/250 mL red kidney beans, precooked or canned

1 cup/250 mL sliced leeks, including part of the green

1 cup/250 mL squash or pumpkin diced into ½-inch (1 cm) cubes

2 cups/500 mL shredded Savoy cabbage

½ cup/125 mL coarsely chopped Italian parsley

extra-virgin olive oil, for garnish

grated cheese of your choice, for garnish

In a stockpot over medium heat, sauté the garlic in the olive oil. Before the garlic browns, add the onion, celery, carrot, zucchini, thyme, bay leaves, and vegetable stock. Simmer for half an hour, or until the vegetables are soft. Season to taste with salt and pepper and add the kidney beans, leeks, squash or pumpkin, and cabbage. Simmer for 15 minutes.

To serve, top with the parsley, a drizzle of olive oil, and a handful of grated cheese of your choice. ☕

minestra di riso e zucca
squash and rice soup

All summer I wait expectantly for the squash or pumpkin plants to bear their fruit. And is it ever worth the wait! I use squash in all sorts of dishes, from risotto to ravioli, from panna cotta to sautéed squash chips. And in soups, of course.

Makes 6–8 servings

1 tbsp/15 mL extra-virgin olive oil	2 bay leaves
1 tbsp/15 mL butter	2 lb/1 kg Hubbard or other dry squash, diced
1 cup/250 mL minced onion	
1 cup/250 mL minced carrot	8 cups/2 L light chicken stock
1 cup/250 mL minced celery	salt and pepper
1 cup/250 mL minced Swiss chard (silverbeet)	2 cups/500 mL vialone nano or other risotto rice
1 tsp/5 mL minced garlic	grated grana padano cheese, for garnish

Heat the olive oil and butter in a large stockpot over medium heat. Add the onion, carrot, celery, Swiss chard (silverbeet), garlic, and bay leaves, and sauté for about 1 minute. Stir in the squash and chicken stock. Simmer for 20 minutes.

Skim off the foam that forms on the top; season the soup to taste with salt and pepper. Add the rice and cook, stirring occasionally to prevent sticking, until tender but still firm, about 14–17 minutes.

Serve in bowls with a generous sprinkling of grated grana padano. ☕

canederli alla trentina
tyrolean bread-dumpling soup

It would be wonderful if we could buy bread fresh every day, but that would probably mean too much left over. In many parts of Italy it is customary not to throw away leftover bread, but to grate it into homemade breadcrumbs, cook it in a custard as bread pudding, add it to soup as a thickening agent, or make it into dumplings, as in this recipe. Serve these dumplings in their cooking broth or with sage butter. Speck is a smoked boneless ham from south Tyrol.

Makes 4 servings

1 lb/500 g stale white bread	pinch of grated nutmeg
1 cup/250 mL milk	salt and pepper
1 tbsp/15 mL butter	5 cups/1.25 L chicken stock
4 oz/115 g speck, chopped	grated Parmigiano-Reggiano cheese, for garnish
3 cloves garlic, chopped	
1 cup/250 mL grated grana padano cheese	
2 eggs	**For sage butter:**
4 tbsp/60 mL chopped Italian parsley	12 whole sage leaves
1 tbsp/15 mL all-purpose (plain) flour	3 tbsp/45 mL butter

Chop the bread into small cubes and place in a medium bowl. Warm the milk and pour it over the bread. Let the bread steep in the milk for at least 2 hours.

Melt the butter in a skillet over medium heat. Add the speck and garlic; sauté gently until soft. Set aside to cool.

Add the grana padano and eggs to the bread mixture. Stir in the parsley, flour, and nutmeg, and season to taste with salt and pepper. Add the speck to the bread mixture and stir well; the mixture should be dough-like, soft and firm for easy handling, and sticky, not runny.

Bring the chicken stock to a gentle boil in a stockpot. In the meantime, dust your hands with flour to prevent sticking and roll the dough between your hands to form dumplings the size of golf balls. Drop the dumplings into the stock and simmer for 20 minutes, stirring occasionally to prevent sticking. Do not cook the dumplings at too rapid a boil or they will fall apart.

To prepare the sage butter, fry the sage leaves in the skillet with the butter until crisp. Add the dumplings, toss to coat, and serve at once with lots of grated Parmigiano-Reggiano.

zemino di ceci
genoa chickpea soup

When I was a boy in the 1960s, chickpeas seemed exotic to me; they are not used in traditional Italian recipes except perhaps as a snack. Sunday afternoons we spent at the cinema. Just before the movie began, an old man on a moped equipped with baskets front and rear would arrive in town to sell popcorn, lupini beans, and steaming hot cooked chickpeas, served salted in a paper cone. My treat was to buy a cola and a cone of chickpeas—nothing tasted as good to me in those days. Today I eat and cook with chickpeas quite often. This hearty soup is particularly nice in the autumn and winter.

Note: Soak the chickpeas overnight in a large bowl of cold water to soften, having first picked them over and discarded any stones or other particles. Rinse well under running water before using.

Makes 6–8 servings

3 cloves garlic, minced

1 cup/250 mL minced carrot

1 cup/250 mL minced celery

1 cup/250 mL minced onion

2 tbsp/30 mL extra-virgin olive oil

2 bay leaves

2 cups/500 mL chopped Swiss chard (silverbeet)

2 cups/500 mL dried chickpeas, presoaked

8 cups/2 L chicken stock

salt and pepper

grated pecorino cheese, for garnish

garlic croutons, for garnish

In a large pot, sauté the garlic, carrot, celery, and onion in the olive oil over medium heat until the vegetables are translucent. Add the bay leaves, Swiss chard (silverbeet), presoaked chickpeas, and stock. Simmer for 1½ hours. Season to taste with salt and pepper.

Serve in bowls with grated pecorino and garlic croutons sprinkled on top.

trippa con fagiolini dell'occhio
beef tripe soup with vegetables

Some people cringe at the thought of eating tripe, while others consider it a delicacy. In Cremona we eat this cold-weather dish mainly in osterie, tavern-like restaurants, as a small snack accompanied by a glass of good red wine. Once a year, at the beginning of autumn, it is a Cremona tradition to eat a bowl of tripe soup for good luck.

Note: Soak the black-eyed peas in cold water overnight. Rinse well under cold running water before using. Alternatively, do a quick soak by bringing the peas to a boil, turning off the heat, and letting stand for 1 hour.

Makes 4–6 servings

1 lb/500 g beef tripe	2 bay leaves
1 vanilla bean	2 tbsp/30 mL tomato paste
4 tbsp/60 mL white vinegar	2 cups/500 mL chopped tomatoes
5 cloves garlic, 4 left whole, 1 minced	6 cups/1.5 L chicken stock
pinch of salt	6 oz/170 g dried black-eyed peas, presoaked
3 tbsp/45 mL extra-virgin olive oil	
1 cup/250 mL minced onion	salt and pepper
1 cup/250 mL minced celery	½ cup/125 mL grated Parmigiano-Reggiano cheese
1 cup/250 mL minced carrot	

Wash the tripe thoroughly under cold running water. Cut into strips no longer than 2 inches (5 cm) and no wider than ½ inch (5 mm). Place the tripe in a pot of water with the vanilla bean, vinegar, 4 whole cloves of garlic, and pinch of salt; simmer for 15 minutes. Remove the tripe and set aside on a tray to cool.

Heat a stockpot over medium-high heat. Add the olive oil, minced garlic, onion, celery, carrot, and bay leaves; sauté for 5 minutes. Add the tripe and tomato paste and cook, stirring, for 1 minute. Stir in the tomatoes, chicken stock, and presoaked peas. Simmer until the tripe and the peas are tender, about 40 minutes. At this point the soup should be quite thick.

Season to taste with salt and pepper. Serve in individual bowls, with grated Parmigiano-Reggiano sprinkled on top, and accompanied by toasted garlic bread.

pasta e fagioli alla veneziana
bean and pasta soup venetian style

My father would eat romano beans only if they were shelled and skinned, which kept my mother busy for hours. You'll see that my father has greatly influenced this recipe—the beans don't need to be skinned. I recommend using fresh romano beans if they are available.

Makes 6–8 servings

2 tbsp/30 mL olive oil

2 tbsp/30 mL butter

2 cloves garlic, minced

2 cups/500 mL minced onion

1 cup/250 mL chopped pancetta

2 bay leaves

2 tbsp/30 mL tomato paste

8 cups/2 L light chicken stock, plus more as needed

2 lb/1 kg fresh romano beans (or 3 cups/750 mL drained canned romano beans)

salt and pepper

½ lb/250 g fresh fettuccine, cut into 2-inch (5 cm) pieces

extra-virgin olive oil, for garnish

grated grana padano cheese, for garnish

Heat the oil and butter in a cast-iron or other heavy-bottomed pot over medium heat. Add the garlic, onion, pancetta, and bay leaves, and sauté until the vegetables are soft and translucent. Stir in the tomato paste and cook a minute longer. Add the beans and stock, and simmer until the beans are cooked (about 20–30 minutes for fresh beans) or heated through (if using canned beans).

Scoop the beans out of the liquid and remove the bay leaves. Puree the beans in a food mill or food processor. Return the pureed beans to the stock and bring to a boil. The soup should be creamy but not too thick; add a bit of stock to thin it if necessary. Season to taste with salt and pepper.

Add the fettuccine and simmer, stirring frequently, until the pasta is cooked. Serve in bowls with a drizzle of olive oil and grated grana padano sprinkled on top. 🍲

insalate e uova / salads and eggs

"sfricasot" di mio papa
my father's scrambled eggs

My father loved preparing this dish, and it is one of the first dishes I learned to cook. It's simple to prepare—perfect after a long day at work or for a relaxed breakfast. These eggs are top of the line; they go well with smoked salmon, on toast with shaved truffle, or as a teaser with caviar, but also with a simple side salad.

Makes 4 servings

6 eggs	salt and pepper to taste
½ cup/125 mL grated Parmigiano-Reggiano cheese	1 tsp/5 mL olive oil
¼ cup/50 mL heavy cream	1 tsp/5 mL butter

Break the eggs into a bowl. Stir in the Parmigiano-Reggiano and cream. Season to taste with the salt and pepper.

Heat the olive oil and butter in a skillet (or use a nonstick skillet with no oil if you prefer) and pour in the egg mixture. With a heat-resistant spatula, scramble the eggs gently until cooked; they should be fluffy and light.

mortadella croccante all'occhio di bue
fried egg with crispy mortadella

If you like to play the "one-up" game with your food, try this instead of bacon and eggs. I don't need to tell you to buy the best Italian-style mortadella you can find, do I?

Makes 4 servings

1 tbsp/15 mL extra-virgin olive oil

1 large slice of mortadella,
½ inch (5 mm) thick

4 eggs

pepper

Heat the olive oil in a skillet over medium heat (or use a nonstick skillet with no oil if you prefer). Place the slice of mortadella in the pan and fry for about 1 minute, or until it starts to turn golden and crispy at the edges.

Flip the mortadella and immediately break the eggs on top of it. Season with pepper to taste and cover the pan with a lid, checking occasionally to make sure the mortadella isn't burning. Cook the eggs to your liking, and serve at once.

frittata di mia mamma
my mother's frittata

If you go to Cremona, you may notice that the locals follow a routine: at about 11:00 AM they stop to have a snack and a glass of white wine or an aperitif. One of the many offerings at the bars is frittata. There is an art to frittata, and when it is made well, it can be difficult to stop at just one bite. Here is my mother's recipe.

Makes 8 servings

3 cups/750 mL spinach	1 cup/250 mL grated mild provolone cheese
3 cups/750 mL Swiss chard (silverbeet)	salt and pepper
2 green zucchini	2 tbsp/30 mL extra-virgin olive oil
12 eggs	2 tbsp/30 mL butter
1 cup/250 mL grated Parmigiano-Reggiano cheese	1 clove garlic, minced
	2 cups/500 mL julienned onion

Preheat oven to 350°F (180°C).

Wash the spinach and the Swiss chard (silverbeet) well, and boil or steam until tender. Squeeze out the excess water and chop coarsely. Cut the zucchini in half lengthwise and then into half-moons.

Break the eggs into a bowl and combine with the spinach, Swiss chard (silverbeet), Parmigiano-Reggiano, and provolone, mixing well to combine the eggs and loosen up the greens. Season to taste with salt and pepper.

Over medium heat, heat an oven-proof skillet; a 12-inch (30 cm) nonstick pan works best—you want the frittata to be at least 1½ inches (4 cm) thick. Add the olive oil and butter, zucchini, garlic, and onion, and sauté until the vegetables are soft and translucent. Add the egg mixture and stir well to incorporate it into the zucchini-onion mixture.

Place the pan in the oven and bake until the frittata is firm, about 10 minutes. The eggs are done when a toothpick inserted in the center of the frittata comes out dry.

Slide the frittata onto a plate, cut into wedges, and serve at once.

insalata di primavera
spring salad with asparagus, fiddleheads, and hazelnut vinaigrette

Springtime is the season for fiddleheads (fern shoots), ramp (wild garlic), asparagus, and peas. If you can't find fiddleheads, add some more asparagus, and cloves of garlic can be used instead of ramp.

Makes 4–6 servings

1 bunch white asparagus, tips only	1 cup/250 mL finely sliced shiitake mushrooms
1 bunch green asparagus, tips only	salt and pepper
1½ cups/375 mL fiddleheads, cleaned well	2 tbsp/30 mL sherry vinegar
1 cup/250 mL shelled fresh green peas	2 heads blond frisée (coral lettuce) or curly endive
1 bunch mini carrots, peeled	1 tbsp/15 mL hazelnut oil
1 tbsp/15 mL butter	2 tbsp/30 mL grapeseed oil
8 whole ramp, coarsely chopped	2 tbsp/30 mL toasted hazelnuts, for garnish

Steam or boil the asparagus tips, fiddleheads, green peas, and carrots.

Heat the butter in a skillet over medium heat. Add the ramp and mushrooms and sauté for 2 minutes. Season with salt and pepper, sprinkle with the sherry vinegar, and cook for 1 minute. Set aside.

Separate the lettuce leaves in a bowl. Add the steamed vegetables and the ramp-and-mushroom mixture. Whisk the hazelnut and grapeseed oils and season with salt and pepper. Dress the salad and arrange on individual plates. Top with cracked hazelnuts.

insalata di alberto
al's plaid salad

The idea of creating recipes to honor people, events, or places is not new. Although I can't remember exactly why, I know that this salad was created at Prego della Piazza for a play called *Forever Plaid* and named for Alberto, a very dear friend. The look and flavor combination of its ingredients is probably the reason why this salad always remained on the menu.

Makes 4–6 servings

1 cup/250 mL coarse sea salt	1 tbsp/15 mL red vine vinegar
1 white onion, skin left on	1 tbsp/15 mL vincotto vinegar
1 head radicchio	¼ cup/50 mL extra-virgin olive oil
2 bunches arugula (rocket)	salt and pepper
2 tomatoes	
1 cup/250 mL canned cannellini beans	

Preheat oven to 375°F (190°C).

Spread the sea salt over the bottom of an ovenproof dish, place the onion on top, and bake for 30–45 minutes.

Julienne the radicchio into ½-inch (5 mm) pieces and place in a serving bowl. Wash and dry the arugula (rocket) and add to the radicchio. Cut the tomatoes in half and remove the seeds, julienne into ½-inch (5 mm) pieces, and add to the bowl. Peel and julienne the baked onion and add to the bowl. Add the cannellini beans.

Whisk together the red wine vinegar, vincotto vinegar, olive oil, and salt and pepper. Dress the salad to taste, tossing well.

insalata d'autunno
autumn salad with radicchio, red onion, and crispy shallots

Autumn is my favorite season in many ways. The scorching heat of summer is gone, the sun sets earlier, the fields yield the final harvest of the year, and the markets are filled with produce from local farms. This tasty salad calls for some of the best of the season's produce. It doesn't take a lot of time to prepare and it's sure to please. Sometimes I shave Parmigiano or asiago on top and have a bowl for lunch—it usually keeps me going until dinnertime.

Note: If you prefer, buy the shallots already fried; they're readily available in Asian markets and the Asian food section of supermarkets.

Makes 4–6 servings

For pickled red onion:

1 cup/250 mL water

1 cup/250 mL red wine vinegar

½ tsp/5 mL salt

1 tbsp/15 mL honey

2 medium red onions, julienned

For crispy shallots:

12 shallots, thinly sliced

4 tbsp/60 mL all-purpose (plain) flour

4 cups/1 L vegetable oil

pinch of salt

For salad:

½ head radicchio, julienned

1 Belgian endive, julienned

½ head escarole, julienned

1 medium blond frisée (coral lettuce), with bottom cut off to separate leaves

1 unpeeled green apple, julienned

1 cup/250 mL julienned carrots

2 plum (Roma) tomatoes, peeled, seeded, and julienned

2 tbsp/30 mL julienned pickled or raw red onion

4 tbsp/60 mL apple cider vinegar

4 tbsp/60 mL extra-virgin olive oil

salt and pepper

2 tbsp/30 mL toasted almonds

To prepare the pickled red onion, bring the water, red wine vinegar, salt, and honey to a boil in a small saucepan. Stir in the onion and bring back to a boil. Remove from the heat and let steep for 5 minutes. Strain and set aside, covered, until needed.

To prepare the crispy shallots, dredge the shallots in flour. Heat the vegetable oil to 285°F (140°C) and fry the shallots until crisp. Remove from the oil with a slotted spoon and drain on paper towels. Sprinkle with a pinch of salt.

To prepare the salad, toss together the radicchio, Belgian endive, escarole, blond frisée (coral lettuce), apple, carrot, tomato, and pickled or raw red onion in a bowl. Whisk together the apple cider vinegar, olive oil, salt, and pepper. Dress the salad to taste and toss well. Top with the crispy shallots and toasted almonds.

insalata d'estate
summer salad

Nothing beats a salad on a hot summer day—the ingredients are plentiful and at their prime, the combinations endless. I love to eat a big salad for dinner in the backyard with my feet up, watching the birds and waiting for the sunset. But, given the business I'm in, that's a rare occurrence, as summer is a busy season for the restaurant. Nevertheless, I still eat my summer salad.

Makes 4–6 servings

1 big handful French green beans (approximately 24)	1 cucumber, cut in half lengthwise, seeds removed
1 head Boston lettuce	4 tbsp/60 mL extra-virgin olive oil
1 head red leaf lettuce	1 tbsp/15 mL red wine vinegar
6 red radishes, thinly sliced	salt and pepper
4 green onions, chopped	1 avocado, peeled, pitted, and diced
2 medium carrots, finely julienned	2 tbsp/30 mL crumbled feta cheese (optional)
2 red tomatoes, cut in wedges	garlic croutons, for garnish

Boil the French beans in a pot of salted water to desired tenderness. In the meantime, toss together the Boston lettuce, red leaf lettuce, radishes, green onions, carrots, tomatoes, and cucumber in a large bowl. Add the cooked French beans.

Whisk together the olive oil, red wine vinegar, and salt and pepper to taste. Dress the salad, tossing lightly (spoons or clean hands, rather than tongs, work best), and divide onto individual plates. Top each with the avocado, crumbled feta, and hand-crumbled garlic croutons.

insalata belga e formaggio verde
belgian endive, roquefort, and pecan salad with pear vinaigrette

Makes 4 servings

For salad:

8 oz/225 g green beans

1 medium red onion

salt and pepper

extra-virgin olive oil, for seasoning

2 Belgian endives

1 bunch arugula (rocket)

2 Bosc pears, peeled, cored, and diced

8 oz/225 g crumbled Roquefort cheese

4 tbsp/60 mL toasted pecans or walnuts

For vinaigrette:

1 Bosc pear, peeled, cored, and diced

2 tbsp/30 mL rice vinegar

6 tbsp/90 mL light extra-virgin olive oil

salt and pepper

Preheat oven to 400°F (200°C).

Bring a pot of water to a boil. Add the green beans and cook until crisp-tender. Remove the beans and plunge into cold water to retain their color. Set aside.

Cut the onion in half crosswise and season with salt, pepper, and olive oil. Bake until tender, about 20 minutes. Set aside to cool, then cut into wedges.

Separate the endive leaves and mix with the arugula (rocket). Add the cooked green beans, onion wedges, pear, Roquefort, and pecans or walnuts.

For the vinaigrette, blend the pear, rice vinegar, olive oil, and salt and pepper to taste in a blender at high speed. Pour over the salad, toss well, and serve.

insalata d'invèrno
winter salad with potatoes and apples

One day, many years ago, I got tired of making "spring mix" salad in winter, so I yanked the Caesar and mesclun salads from the menu and started making salads by the season. Doing so gave the kitchen a boost of creativity. This is one of the many combinations we created.

Note: Soak the radicchio in cold water overnight to remove bitterness.

Makes 4–6 servings

2 large potatoes	2 heads radicchio, washed and cut into small pieces
salt and pepper	2 tbsp/30 mL chopped Italian parsley
4 tbsp/60 mL cider vinegar	½ cup/125 mL shaved asiago cheese, for garnish
2 crisp green apples	2 tbsp/30 mL crispy bacon bits, for garnish
juice of 1 lemon	
4 tbsp/60 mL extra-virgin olive oil	
1 small sweet onion, julienned	

Cook the potatoes, skin on, in salted boiling water under fork-tender. Once they are cool enough to handle, remove the skins and dice the potatoes into 1-inch (2.5 cm) cubes. Dress immediately with salt, pepper, and 2 tbsp/30 mL cider vinegar. Dressing the potatoes while they are warm will make them very flavorful (this process can be done the day before if you wish).

Cut the apples into wide juliennes and sprinkle with lemon juice to prevent discoloring.

Heat 1 tbsp/15 mL olive oil in a skillet over high heat. Add the onion and toss rapidly to prevent scorching. Sprinkle with the remaining 2 tbsp/30 mL cider vinegar, cook for 2 minutes, and remove from heat.

In a medium bowl combine the potatoes, apples, radicchio, and parsley. Pour the onion-and-vinegar mixture on top and dress with salt, pepper, and the remaining 3 tbsp/45 mL olive oil, tossing gently to blend the flavors. To finish, divide the salad into individual bowls and sprinkle with shaved asiago and bacon bits.

panzanella toscana
tuscan bread salad

I spent five summers by the Tuscan seaside working in a small hotel. There I developed a friendship with the baker who supplied bread to the hotel. This very generous man frequently invited me to his house for a grigliata al fresco, or outdoor grill, where the wine flowed and the food was plentiful. It was here that I first tasted panzanella. Made with stale bread, this salad can be prepared ahead of time—great for picnics and summer buffets in the garden.

Makes 4–6 servings

1 lb/500 g chopped ripe tomatoes	4 tbsp/60 mL extra-virgin olive oil
1 cucumber, peeled, seeded, and chopped	2 tbsp/30 mL red wine vinegar
1 medium red onion, julienned	salt and pepper
1 large bunch basil	1 loaf crusty Italian bread, preferably stale
1 bunch mint	

Combine the tomatoes and cucumber in a bowl. Add the onion and the basil and mint leaves. Dress the tomato mixture with the olive oil, red wine vinegar, and salt and pepper to taste. Break the bread into small pieces by hand and add to the salad. Toss well and serve.

insalata rossa
red salad

When I worked at Prego della Piazza, I was inspired by famed restaurateur Michael Carlevale. His passion for his craft was the drive behind every aspect of his life. "My customers," he explained to me, "are my guests, and this restaurant is my living room." Those were very good—but long—days. The restaurant opened at 11:30 AM and closed when the last guests had left, sometimes in the wee hours of the morning. On the menu were many salads, and this is one of the most popular. If radicchio di Treviso is unavailable, substitute red radicchio.

Makes 4 servings

2 medium beetroots	1 head radicchio di Treviso, chopped
2 red onions	8 soft oil-packed sun-dried tomatoes
salt	4 slices red tomato
extra-virgin olive oil, for seasoning	4 tbsp/60 mL extra-virgin olive oil
1 tsp/5 mL red vine vinegar	4 tsp/20 mL good balsamic vinegar
2 red peppers (capsicums), quartered	flaked sea salt and freshly ground black pepper

Preheat oven to 450°F (230°C).

Boil the beetroots in a pot of salted water until they are soft, about 30 minutes. Cool and peel. Slice crosswise into $\frac{1}{2}$-inch (5 mm) slices and set aside.

Cut the onions in half crosswise and season with salt and a light sprinkling of olive oil—just enough to give the onions a shine. Place the onions on a small baking sheet and bake until soft, about 20 minutes. Remove from the oven and sprinkle with the red wine vinegar. Set aside to cool.

Turn the oven up to 500°F (260°C). Give the peppers (capsicums) a light sprinkling of olive oil and place them on the baking sheet; bake for about 15 minutes. Remove the peppers (capsicums) and put them in a plastic bag to steam; this will make removing the skins easy once they are cold.

To prepare the salad, arrange the radicchio on individual serving plates. Add, from right to left, the tomato slices, roasted peppers (capsicums), sun-dried tomatoes, beetroots, and roasted onions. To dress, sprinkle each salad with 1 tbsp/15 mL olive oil and 1 tsp/5 mL balsamic vinegar, sea salt, and freshly ground black pepper to taste.

risotto e polenta /
risotto and polenta

risotto ubriaco
drunken risotto

If you have heard of champagne risotto, then you will understand this recipe. I first encountered it in a restaurant in Venice, where it was made with Amarone. At first I thought it a waste of good wine, until I learned that using only the best-quality ingredients when preparing a recipe is as important as having the right drinking wine to accompany the dish.

Makes 4–6 servings

1 onion, finely chopped	2 cups/500 mL full-bodied red wine
4 cloves garlic, thinly sliced	6 cups/1.5 L light chicken stock
2 tbsp/30 mL vegetable oil	2 tbsp/30 mL butter
1 cup/250 mL smoked pork belly, diced into $\frac{1}{2}$-inch (5 mm) pieces	4 tbsp/60 mL grated Parmigiano-Reggiano cheese
$3\frac{1}{2}$ cups/875 mL carnaroli rice, unwashed	

Sweat the onion and garlic in the vegetable oil. Add the diced pork belly and stir to mix well.

Add the rice and toast it, stirring constantly to prevent sticking, for 2–3 minutes, until it is very hot but not browned. Pour in the wine and simmer until the liquid is absorbed or evaporated. Add enough chicken stock to cover the rice; simmer until the rice has absorbed most of the liquid, stirring frequently to prevent sticking. Continue to add the stock, a ladleful at a time, letting the rice absorb most of the liquid before adding more, until the rice is tender but firm. Be careful toward the end not to add too much stock—the risotto should be creamy, not soupy. This process should take 16–18 minutes in total.

When the rice is cooked, remove from the heat. Add the butter and Parmigiano-Reggiano; stir vigorously to fluff. Serve at once in bowls.

risotto con asparagi bianchi, pepe nero e fragole
risotto with white asparagus, black pepper, and wild strawberries

The most important thing to remember when making risotto is to introduce a flavor that complements the rice—in this case, asparagus and strawberries. Don't worry about the asparagus not being crunchy; the more you cook it, the tastier it will be. Choose soft, fragrant strawberries. Feel free to use white or wild asparagus when in season.

Makes 4–6 servings

1 medium onion, finely chopped	2 cups/500 mL ripe strawberries, diced
2 tbsp/30 mL extra-virgin olive oil	2 tbsp/30 mL butter
1 bunch asparagus, cleaned, blanched, and diced	grated Parmesan cheese
3½ cups/875 mL carnaroli rice, unwashed	grated zest of 1 lemon
½ cup/125 mL white wine	aged balsamic vinegar, for garnish
6 cups/1.5 L chicken or vegetable stock, preferably with an asparagus flavor	

In a heavy-bottomed pot over medium heat, sauté the onion in the olive oil. Add the asparagus and sauté for 2–3 minutes. Add the rice and toast it, stirring constantly to prevent sticking, for 2–3 minutes, until it is very hot but not browned.

Pour in the wine and simmer until it is absorbed or evaporated. Add two ladlefuls of stock and simmer gently, stirring frequently to prevent sticking, until the rice has absorbed most of the liquid. Continue adding the stock, a ladleful at a time, letting the rice absorb most of the liquid before adding more, until the rice is tender but firm. Be careful toward the end not to add too much stock—the risotto should be creamy, not soupy. This process should take 16–18 minutes in total.

When the rice is cooked, remove from the heat. Add the strawberries, butter, Parmesan, and lemon zest. Stir well and serve with aged balsamic vinegar drizzled around the edges.

risotto e polenta   risotto and polenta

risotto alle erbette e pecorino
herbed risotto with pecorino

For this risotto, the amount of greens you use will greatly affect the taste. For me, the more the better. The pecorino pepato (sheep's milk cheese with whole peppercorns) will also influence the taste, so use restraint when adding it.

Makes 4–6 servings

6 cups/1.5 L vegetable stock

1 onion, finely chopped

4 cloves garlic, crushed

2 tbsp/30 mL extra-virgin olive oil

2 bunches baby spinach, chopped

2 bunches Swiss chard (silverbeet), greens only, chopped

$3\frac{1}{2}$ cups/875 mL vialone nano or other risotto rice, unwashed

$\frac{1}{2}$ cup/125 mL white wine

2 tbsp/30 mL butter

$\frac{1}{2}$ cup/125 mL grated pecorino pepato cheese

Bring the stock to a boil, turn down the heat, and keep it at a simmer.

In a large sauté pan over medium heat, sweat the onion and garlic with the olive oil. Add the spinach and Swiss chard (silverbeet) and sauté until all the liquid has evaporated.

Add the rice, stir to coat, and let it toast for 2–3 minutes, stirring constantly. Pour in the wine and stir until it is absorbed or evaporated.

Add a ladleful of vegetable stock and stir frequently until the rice has absorbed most of the liquid. Continue adding the stock a ladleful at a time, letting the rice absorb most of the liquid before adding more, until the rice is tender but firm. Be careful not to let the rice dry out too much, but also be careful toward the end not to add too much stock—the risotto should be creamy, not soupy. This process should take 16–18 minutes in total.

When the rice is cooked, remove it from the heat. Add the butter and pecorino; stir vigorously to fluff. Serve immediately in bowls. ☜

risotto alle rape rosse
red beet risotto

I began developing this recipe back in the 1980s at Prego della Piazza. My partner, Michael Carlevale, and I were experimenting with colored foods—red, green, yellow, orange. Making risotto has always been one of my strong suits, so the dish was a natural candidate for such experiments. Beetroots are one of my favourite vegetables, and so the recipe was born.

Makes 4–6 servings

2 cups/500 mL beetroot juice	3½ cups/875 mL carnaroli rice
1 onion, finely chopped	½ cup/125 mL white wine
4 cloves garlic, thinly sliced	4 cups/1 L vegetable stock
2 tbsp/30 mL vegetable oil	2 tbsp/30 mL butter
1 bunch beetroot greens, finely chopped	4 tbsp/60 mL grated Parmigiano-Reggiano cheese

Bring the beetroot juice to a boil and skim off the foam. Set aside to cool.

In a medium saucepan over medium heat, sauté the onion and garlic in the vegetable oil. Add the beetroot greens and stir well. Add the rice and stir to coat with the onion mixture.

Pour in the wine and stir until most of the liquid is absorbed or evaporated. Add about half the stock, a ladleful at a time, and simmer until the rice has absorbed most of it, stirring frequently to prevent sticking. Add the beetroot juice, 1 cup/250 mL at a time, and simmer until the rice has absorbed most of it. Continue adding stock one ladleful at a time. Be careful not to add too much stock; the risotto should be creamy, not soupy, and the rice should be tender but firm. This process should take 16–18 minutes in total.

When the rice is cooked, remove it from the heat and add the butter and Parmigiano-Reggiano. Serve at once in bowls.

polenta taragna
buckwheat and cheese polenta

North of Cremona lies the town of Bergamo. Bergamo's historic center is divided in two—the very old high city and the more modern lower city. You'll find top-notch restaurants and trattorie with wonderful local foods; my wife and I had this polenta dish in one of them and we absolutely loved it. Serve it with steamed vegetables or sautéed porcini mushrooms, or as a side dish with a pot roast or stew.

Makes 6–8 servings

4 cups/1 L water

salt

2 tbsp/30 mL extra-virgin olive oil

2 cups/500 mL coarse buckwheat flour

1 cup/250 mL yellow cornmeal polenta flour (preferably bergamasca)

2 cups/500 mL Bitto or casera cheese

2 tbsp/30 mL grated Parmigiano-Reggiano cheese

2 tbsp/30 mL stracchino cheese

Combine the buckwheat and polenta flours. In a medium pot, bring the water to a boil, salt to taste, and add the oil. Reduce the heat to low and gently whisk in the flours, adding as much as needed to make a paste-like consistency.

Simmer gently, stirring occasionally, for about 45 minutes. Remove from the heat and add the cheeses, stirring vigorously until the cheese becomes stringy. Serve at once. 🍲

risotto con zucchine e scampi
scampi and zucchini risotto

Even though this is a seafood risotto, I like to use a light chicken stock. It makes the rice creamy and accentuates the flavors of the other ingredients, rather than masking them. I have tried using fish stock, but find the taste too strong.

Note: Zucchini can be pulpy, so I recommend slicing them in half lengthwise and scooping out the seeds before slicing them into half-moons.

Makes 4–6 servings

6 cups/1.5 L light chicken stock

12 oz/340 g scampi

1 cup/250 mL chopped onion

1 clove garlic, chopped

2 cups/500 mL zucchini, sliced into ½-inch (5 mm) half-moons

2 tbsp/30 mL extra-virgin olive oil

3½ cups/875 mL carnaroli rice, unwashed

1 cup/250 mL white wine

2 tbsp/30 mL butter

1 bunch Italian parsley, chopped

¼ cup/50 mL asiago cheese

Bring the chicken stock to a boil. Meanwhile, shell and devein the scampi, reserving the shells. Once the stock has reached a boil, add the scampi shells and simmer.

In a heavy-bottomed pot over medium heat, sauté the onion, garlic, and zucchini in the olive oil until the vegetables are soft. Add the scampi and sauté lightly. Add the rice and let it toast for 2–3 minutes, stirring constantly to prevent sticking, until very hot but not browned.

Pour in the white wine and simmer until the liquid is absorbed or evaporated. Add two ladlefuls of chicken stock (without the scampi shells) and simmer gently, stirring occasionally to prevent sticking, until the rice has absorbed most of the liquid. Continue adding the stock, a ladleful at a time, letting the rice absorb most of the liquid before adding more, until the rice is tender but firm. Be careful toward the end not to add too much stock—the risotto should be creamy and dense, not soupy. This process should take 16–18 minutes in total.

When the rice is cooked, remove it from the heat and add the butter, parsley, and asiago. Stir well and serve.

risotto e polenta   risotto and polenta

polenta di castagne
chestnut polenta

October in Italy brings many festivals, most of them related to the autumn harvest of mushrooms, truffles, pumpkins, grapes, and, of course, chestnuts. I like to boil chestnuts and simply peel and eat them. Others in my family like them roasted.

This polenta is made with chestnut flour. Your local Italian food shop should carry it; if it doesn't, ask to have it brought in. This polenta has a sweet flavor and there are many ways to serve it. Try it with sautéed mushrooms or crispy bacon and fresh goat cheese or sautéed Brussels sprouts, cabbage, and pork or wild game stew.

Makes 4 servings

4 cups/1 L water

½ tsp/2 mL salt

1 tbsp/15 mL extra-virgin olive oil

1½ cups/425 mL chestnut flour, sifted

Bring the water, salt, and olive oil to a boil. Remove from heat and gently add the sifted flour, whisking constantly to prevent lumps. Once all the flour is incorporated, return the pot to the heat and simmer over low heat, stirring occasionally, for 10–15 minutes.

polenta di ceci "panella"
fried chickpea polenta

Panella is a Sicilian snack food that can be found in just about any friggitoria, or shop that specializes in fried foods. I first encountered it in my army days, when my Sicilian friends made it. Eat it between sliced bread with a sprinkling of salt or dressed with tomatoes and olive spread. Once fried, it can be used as a side dish with lamb or fish, or make it into croutons for salads instead of using bread.

Makes 26 panelle

3 cups/750 mL water	2 tbsp/30 mL minced Italian parsley
2½ cups/625 mL chickpea flour	2 tbsp/30 mL dried oregano
salt and pepper	6 cups/1.5 L vegetable oil

Pour the water into a medium saucepan and stir in the chickpea flour, whisking to break up any lumps. Season to taste with salt and pepper and cook over medium heat, stirring constantly, for about 15 minutes, until the mixture begins to pull away from the sides of the pan. Add the parsley and oregano and pour the mixture onto an oiled cookie sheet, spreading it out with a spatula to ½ inch (5 mm) thick. Set aside to cool completely, then cut into 2x3-inch (5x8 cm) rectangles.

In a frying pan, heat the vegetable oil to 375°F (190°C) and fry the polenta in batches; don't put too many in at one time, as that will lower the temperature of the oil. Fry until the panelle are golden brown, turning as necessary. Remove from the oil with a slotted spoon and drain on paper towels. Serve at once.

purè di fave e cicoria
fava bean polenta with chicory

Many years ago I visited the region of Puglia, on the heel of Italy. It was my first time there, and it was a great eating experience. Puglia is known for fruits and vegetables of all sorts, especially its olives. The region is surrounded by the sea and has terrific restaurants. One, in the town of Alberobello, served this dish accompanied by grilled country-style crusty bread, olive oil, and black olives. It was delicious in its simplicity.

Makes 4–6 servings

12 oz/340 g dried fava (broad) beans, soaked overnight

8 oz/225 g potatoes, peeled and diced

salt

1 lb/500 g fresh chicory or dandelion greens, chopped

1 cup/250 mL extra-virgin olive oil

¼ cup/175 mL infornate (baked) black olives, pitted

extra-virgin olive oil, for garnish

freshly ground black pepper

Place the soaked beans and potatoes in a saucepan. Add enough water to just cover the vegetables, season with ¼ tsp/2 mL salt, and bring to a boil. Lower the heat and simmer gently for about 15 minutes, checking occasionally and adding more water if the pan becomes too dry. The potatoes are cooked when soft, and the beans when they are falling apart.

Mash the bean-and-potato mixture with a wooden spoon or potato masher. Season to taste with salt.

Bring the chicory to a boil in salted water and cook for about 1 minute. Drain and add it to the mashed beans and potato.

Place one spoonful of the bean mixture on a plate and spread it out to cover the surface. Garnish with the olives and a generous pour of olive oil. Top with freshly ground black pepper and serve warm.

risotto e polenta   risotto and polenta

risotto con radicchio, pancetta e vincotto
risotto with radicchio, bacon, and vincotto

Why use radicchio only in salads? If you are concerned it will be too bitter, soak cleaned, cut radicchio overnight in cold water to remove the bitterness. There are several varieties of radicchio; the radicchio di Treviso called for in this recipe looks like red Belgian endive. You may substitute red radicchio if radicchio di Treviso is unavailable.

Pancetta is the Italian name for salt-cured bacon; it comes rolled or flat, roasted or smoked, double-smoked, or in many other forms. For this recipe, choose pancetta affumicata, or roasted bacon, which can be found in the deli section of most supermarkets. It is similar to regular bacon but contains less water.

Makes 4–6 servings

1 medium onion, finely chopped	$3\frac{1}{2}$ cups/875 mL vialone nano or other risotto rice, unwashed
8 oz/225 g pancetta affumicata (roasted bacon), cut into $\frac{1}{2}$-inch (1 cm) pieces	$\frac{1}{2}$ cup/125 mL white wine
	6 cups/1.5 L chicken stock
3 cups/750 mL diced radicchio di Treviso	2 tbsp/30 mL butter
	2 oz/50 g asiago cheese, grated
2 tbsp/30 mL vegetable oil	4 tbsp/60mL vincotto vinegar

In a heavy-bottomed pot over medium heat, sauté the onion, pancetta, and radicchio in the vegetable oil until soft.

Add the rice and toast it, stirring constantly to prevent sticking, for 2–3 minutes, until very hot but not browned. Pour in the wine and simmer until the liquid is absorbed or evaporated. Add two ladlefuls of chicken stock and simmer gently, stirring frequently to prevent sticking. Continue adding the stock, a ladleful at a time, letting the rice absorb most of the liquid before adding more, until the rice is tender but firm. Be careful toward the end not to add too much stock—the risotto should be creamy, not soupy. This process should take 16–18 minutes in total.

When the rice is cooked, remove it from the heat and add the butter and asiago. Spoon into bowls, drizzle 1 tbsp/15 mL of vincotto over each, and serve at once. 🍲

risotto e polenta　　　　　　　　　　　　risotto and polenta

risotto del contadino
farmer's risotto

Try this recipe and you will learn my idea of comfort food. Risotto is not only tasty, it sticks to your ribs. This recipe in particular is very popular in my house. Don't add too much sausage—the idea is to eat a tasty risotto with a bit of meat in it, not sausage with rice on the side.

Makes 4–6 servings

6 cups/1.5 L chicken stock

1 small onion, finely chopped

2 tbsp/30 mL extra-virgin olive oil

7 oz/200 g sweet Italian sausage, skinned and crumbled

3$\frac{1}{2}$ cups/875 mL vialone nano or other risotto rice, unwashed

$\frac{1}{2}$ cup/125 mL white wine

$\frac{1}{3}$ cup/75 mL tomatoes, skinned, seeded, and diced into $\frac{1}{4}$-inch (5 mm) pieces

2 tbsp/30 mL butter

1 bunch Italian parsley, coarsely chopped

$\frac{1}{2}$ cup/125 mL grated grana padano cheese

Bring the chicken stock to a boil, then reduce heat to simmer.

In a large sauté pan over medium heat, sauté the onion in the olive oil. Add the sausage meat and rice and toast the rice for 2–3 minutes, stirring constantly to prevent sticking, until it is very hot but not browned. Pour in the white wine and simmer, stirring constantly, until the liquid is absorbed or evaporated.

As you continue to stir, add the chicken stock a ladleful at a time, each time letting the rice absorb most of the liquid before adding more. After about 10 minutes, add the tomatoes. Continue adding the stock a ladleful at a time, letting the rice absorb most of the liquid before adding more, until the rice is tender but firm. This process should take 16–18 minutes in total.

When the rice is cooked, remove it from the heat and add the butter, parsley, and grana padano. Stir vigorously, using a whipping motion, to fluff the risotto. Serve at once in bowls.

risotto e polenta   risotto and polenta

bottoni di pagliaccio
grilled polenta "clown's buttons" and sausage

You will have a hard time finding anyone in Cremona who doesn't eat salami. There's a type for every need, and the open-air market is overflowing with stands selling it. This recipe is made with thick Italian sausage and is a favorite in my house, not only because of the taste but also because of its whimsical name—clown's buttons—which is unique to Cremona. We often eat the polenta and sausage by itself as a snack, but it also makes a nice light meal if served with a salad.

Makes 4 servings

2 large Italian sausages	2 scallions, chopped
2 tbsp/30 mL extra-virgin olive oil, plus extra for dressing	1 lb/500 g cooked polenta
6 tbsp/90 mL red vine vinegar, plus extra for dressing	1 head escarole
	salt and pepper

Cut the sausages into coins and sauté in a skillet with 2 tbsp/30 mL of the olive oil until crisp on both sides. Pour in the red wine vinegar and cook until it evaporates. Sprinkle on the scallions and toss briefly to wilt them slightly.

Cut the polenta into disks. Grill or sauté in a pan until crisp on both sides.

Arrange the polenta and sausage coins in rings on a plate, leaving room in the center for the salad. Cut the escarole into bite-sized pieces and season to taste with salt, pepper, olive oil, and vinegar. Place in the center of the plate.☞

risotto all'aragosta
lobster risotto

This risotto is a favorite at Mistura. Of all the ways we have created risotto with lobster, this is definitely my favorite.

Makes 4–6 servings

2 lobsters, weighing 1½ lb/0.5 kg each, or 12 oz/375 g canned or frozen lobster, with juices

8 cups/2 L light chicken stock

2 tbsp/30 mL extra-virgin olive oil

½ cup/125 mL chopped onion

6 fresh plum (Roma) tomatoes, peeled, seeded, and chopped, or 2 cups/500 mL canned tomatoes, chopped and drained

3½ cups/875 mL carnaroli rice, unwashed

½ cup/125 mL white wine

1 bunch basil, chopped

2 tbsp/30 mL butter

If using live lobsters, cook them in boiling salted water for 8 minutes; cool in ice water. Remove the meat and scrape the tomalley (liver) out of the body cavity; reserve the tomalley in a bowl. Cut the meat into ½-inch (1 cm) cubes and set aside.

Meanwhile, bring the chicken stock to a boil and reduce heat to a gentle simmer.

Heat the olive oil in a heavy-bottomed pot over medium heat. Sauté the onion. Add the tomalley and tomatoes; cook for 3–4 minutes. Add the rice and toast it, stirring constantly to prevent sticking, for 2–3 minutes, until it is very hot but not browned.

Pour in the white wine and simmer until the liquid is absorbed or evaporated. Add two ladlefuls of stock and simmer gently, stirring frequently, until the rice has absorbed most of the liquid. Continue adding the stock, a ladleful at a time, keeping the rice wet but letting most of the liquid absorb before adding more, until the rice is tender but firm. Be careful toward the end not to add too much stock—the risotto should be creamy, not soupy. This process should take 16–18 minutes in total.

When the rice is almost cooked, stir in the lobster meat (with juices, if using canned or frozen, for extra flavor to replace the tomalley) and basil. Remove from the heat, stir in the butter, and serve at once in bowls.

risotto e polenta   risotto and polenta

pasta / pasta

bigoli in salsa
spaghetti with anchovies

Bigoli are very thick noodles produced with machines called bigolaro or torchio. Bigoli are know in Italy under many names: in Tuscany they are called pici, farther south spaghettoni or strozzapreti. The sauce originated in Venice and the surrounding region, where it is customary to eat bigoli in salsa on Christmas Eve.

Makes 4–6 servings

1 lb/500 g bigoli or thick spaghetti	2 tbsp/30 mL tomato paste
2 tbsp/30 mL extra-virgin olive oil	2 cups/500 mL chopped, seeded tomatoes
1 medium onion, finely chopped	$\frac{1}{2}$ cup/125 mL water
2 cloves garlic, finely chopped	$\frac{1}{2}$ tsp/5 mL chilli paste
8 oil-packed anchovies, chopped	salt and pepper

Cook the pasta al dente in a big pot of boiling salted water.

In the meantime, heat the oil in a saucepan over medium heat. Sauté the onion for 1 minute. Add the garlic and chopped anchovies, and cook until the vegetables are translucent; the anchovies should break up during this process. Add the tomato paste and cook for 2–3 minutes. Add the tomatoes, water, chilli paste, and salt and pepper to taste, and simmer for about 15 minutes, stirring occasionally.

Drain the cooked pasta and toss with the tomato sauce. Serve at once.

spaghettini ai frutti di mare
spaghettini with seafood

This recipe is a crowd-pleaser. Make sure not to overcook the spaghettini, and let the seafood speak for itself—there's no need for heavy tomato or cream sauces.

Makes 4 servings

8 oz/225 g squid, cleaned (ask your fishmonger to clean it)	¼ cup/50 mL white wine (optional)
1 lb/500 g fresh clams	8 oz/225 g small shrimp, peeled and deveined
1 lb/500 g spaghettini	1 cup/250 mL diced tomatoes
3 tbsp/45 mL extra-virgin olive oil	1 tsp/5 mL dried oregano
1 clove garlic, sliced	salt and pepper
1 onion, finely chopped	4 tbsp/60 mL chopped Italian parsley

Rinse the squid and clams under cold running water to wash off any grit. Slice the squid into very thin rings, about ½ inch (5 mm) thick. Set both aside.

Boil the spaghettini al dente in a big pot of boiling salted water.

In the meantime, heat a skillet over medium heat. Add the oil, garlic, and onion; sauté until the vegetables are soft and translucent. Add the clams and wine, if using, and sauté until the clams have opened, about 3–4 minutes. Discard any clams that do not open.

Add the squid and shrimps and simmer for 1 minute. Stir in the tomatoes, season to taste with oregano, salt, and pepper, and simmer until the sauce has thickened slightly.

Drain the pasta and toss with the sauce. Sprinkle with parsley and serve at once.

ferretti al ragù di carne
handmade noodles with ragu

Despite its Italian name, you won't see any meat in this ragu. After the various meats have been stewed, they are removed to be eaten at another time as a main course. In the north of Italy, meat is boiled to make good stock for tortellini, then removed and served up as bollito misto, literally "boiled dinner."

Ferretti is a pasta made with semolina and hand-rolled into thick, spaghetti-like strips about 3 inches (8 cm) long, using a special tool called a ferretto.

Makes 8 or more servings

2 medium onions, finely chopped	2 cups/500 mL chicken stock
6 cloves garlic, chopped	1 100-oz/2.84 L can crushed tomatoes, the best quality available
½ cup/125 mL extra-virgin olive oil	salt and pepper
1 lb/500 g veal short ribs or brisket	2 bunches basil, chopped
4 Italian sausages, of your choice	2 lb/1 kg ferretti
½ rack pork back ribs	1 tbsp/15 mL butter
½ cup/125 mL white wine	½ cup/125 mL grated provolone cheese, plus more for garnish
1 5.5-oz/156 mL can tomato paste	

In a big pot over medium heat, sauté the onion and garlic in the olive oil until the vegetables are soft and translucent. Add the veal or brisket, sausages, and pork, and brown for 3–4 minutes. Pour in the wine and cook until it evaporates.

Stir in the tomato paste, mixing well, and cook for 1–2 minutes. Add the chicken stock and bring to a gentle simmer. Stir in the tomatoes, season to taste with salt and pepper, add half of the basil, and cook for at least 1½ hours at a very low simmer, stirring occasionally.

Gently remove the meat, which you can serve as a separate meal. Strain the sauce to remove the tomato seeds and other debris; it should be thick and creamy.

Cook the ferretti in plenty of boiling salted water until done to your liking. Drain the pasta and toss with the sauce. Stir in the butter, the remaining basil, and grated provolone to taste. Serve with more provolone for topping.

pizzoccheri della valtellina
buckwheat fettuccine with cabbage, potato, and cheese

This dish is one of the easiest—and tastiest—to make. The cabbage, Swiss chard (silverbeet), and potato balance the coarse texture of the buckwheat. I first had buckwheat fettuccine as a young apprentice working in the Dolomite town of San Martino di Castrozza. I thought it was crazy to pair potatoes with pasta, but I soon realized I had a lot to learn about Italian cuisine!

If you don't wish to make your own pasta, use 1 lb (500 g) store-bought buckwheat fettuccine; many supermarkets, Italian food shops, and health food stores carry it.

Makes 4–6 servings

For pasta:	For sauce:
2½ cups/625 mL fine buckwheat flour	1 large potato
1 cup/250 mL all-purpose (plain) flour	3 cups/750 mL chopped Savoy cabbage
	2 cups/500 mL chopped Swiss chard (silverbeet)
	4 tbsp/60 mL butter
	4 cloves garlic, chopped
	8 sage leaves, chopped
	1 cup/250 mL grated Bitto or casera cheese

To prepare the pasta, mix together the buckwheat and all-purpose (plain) flours in a large bowl. Add enough cool water to make a smooth dough; knead well. Wrap the dough in plastic wrap or cover with a bowl or damp cloth, and let sit for 15 minutes.

Use a pasta roller to make the fettuccine. Don't make the pasta too thin or too long—each strip should be about 6 inches (15 cm) long and no more than ½ inch (5 mm) wide, and just a little thicker than regular fettuccine.

Bring a pot of salted water to a boil. In the meantime, peel and slice the potato into ½-inch (5 mm) pieces. Add the potato to the water and boil for 5 minutes. Add the cabbage, Swiss chard (silverbeet), and pasta, and cook until the pasta is tender, about 2–3 minutes.

When the pasta is almost cooked, melt the butter with the garlic and sage in a large sauté pan over medium heat. Cook until the butter foams slightly.

Drain the pasta and greens and add them to the butter. Toss well, sprinkle the Bitto or casera cheese on top, toss again, and serve at once.

garganelli con le fave e prosciutto

garganelli with fava beans and crispy prosciutto

When you see fresh fava (broad) beans at the market, buy some. The delicious flavor will more than make up for the work of removing the shells and skins. Use them in salads, tossed in oil as a vegetable side dish, or simply boiled and salted as a snack. Or try them in this pasta recipe. Garganelli are small, ridged tubes of pasta. More and more supermarkets are stocking them, but if you're unable to find them, substitute penne.

Makes 4 servings

1 lb/500 g garganelli	12 slices prosciutto, finely sliced
3 tbsp/45 mL extra-virgin olive oil	2 cups/500 mL chopped and seeded fresh plum (Roma) tomatoes
2 cloves garlic, finely chopped	
1 medium onion, finely chopped	1 bunch basil
2 cups/500 mL fava (broad) beans, shelled and skinned	salt and pepper
	Parmigiano-Reggiano cheese, for garnish
1 cup/250 mL vegetable stock	

Cook the pasta in a big pot of boiling salted water. Drain, reserving about 1 cup/250 mL of the cooking water.

In the meantime, heat a saucepan over medium heat. Add 2 tbsp/30 mL of the olive oil, the garlic, and the onion, and cook until the vegetables are soft and translucent. Add the fava (broad) beans and stock; cook until the beans are tender, about 5–6 minutes.

In a skillet over low heat, heat the remaining 1 tbsp/15 mL of olive oil. Cook the prosciutto until crisp, and drain on paper towels.

Add the cooked pasta and tomatoes to the fava (broad) bean mixture and sauté over high heat for 1–2 minutes. Stir in the basil and, if it's too dry, some of the pasta cooking water. Season to taste with salt and pepper.

Serve at once, topped with the fried prosciutto and lots of Parmigiano-Reggiano.

tagliatelle all'aragosta
tagliatelle with lobster sauce

We have a tradition at Mistura: after a busy Saturday night, once all the customers have gone home and we have finished our chores, we head to the local Chinese diner and relax. Over dinner we laugh about the mistakes and misunderstandings of the night. One of the dishes we always order is fried noodles with lobster, ginger, and green onion—the inspiration for this recipe.

Makes 4 servings

1 cup/250 mL leeks, cut in half lengthwise, then in half-circles ½ inch (5 mm) thick	1 clove garlic, crushed
	½ cup/125 mL carrot, finely julienned
1 small bunch green onions	2 tbsp/30 mL white wine
2 1½-lb/625 g lobsters, or 12 oz/ 340 g frozen lobster meat, with juices	1 tbsp/15 mL grated fresh ginger
	salt and pepper
1 lb/500 g tagliatelle, fettuccine, or egg noodles	1 cup/250 mL cherry tomatoes, halved
2 tbsp/30 mL extra-virgin olive oil	2 tbsp/30 mL butter

Rinse the leeks under cold running water to remove any remaining sand; pat dry.

Chop the green onions as finely as possible; include about half of the green part.

If you are using fresh lobster, shell the lobsters and remove the tomalley (liver) and reserve. Cube the lobster meat and set aside. If you are using frozen lobster meat, retain about 4 tbsp/60 mL of the juices that come out of the meat when it thaws, to replace the tomalley.

Cook the pasta al dente in a big pot of boiling salted water, about 5–7 minutes.

In the meantime, heat the olive oil in a skillet over medium heat and sauté the leeks and garlic until soft. Add the carrot, lobster tomalley, and wine. As soon as the wine evaporates, add the lobster meat and then the ginger. Season to taste with salt and pepper.

Add the green onions and cherry tomatoes to the sauce and simmer for 1 minute. Add the cooked pasta and toss. Stir in the butter and serve at once.

couscous perlato al ragù di dentice
pearl couscous in red snapper stew

I developed this recipe at Prego della Piazza for a special dinner honoring Greek wines. I wanted to give the couscous a strong Mediterranean feel, and the result was excellent. This recipe can easily be modified for risotto or white polenta, or keep the fillet whole and serve it as a main course.

Makes 4 servings

12 oz/340 g red snapper fillet	1 cup/250mL pearl (Israeli) couscous
1 medium onion, finely chopped	sea salt and pepper
1 clove garlic, sliced	1 small bunch fresh oregano, finely chopped
2 tbsp/30 mL extra-virgin olive oil	
½ cup/125 mL white wine	juice of ½ lemon
2 cups/500 mL tomato juice	zest of 1 lemon, finely grated
2 cups/500 mL water	1 hot chilli pepper, chopped

Carefully remove the skin and bones from the snapper and set the fillet aside.

In a saucepan over medium heat, sauté the onion and garlic in the olive oil until the vegetables are translucent. Add the snapper and cook gently for 3–4 minutes.

Pour in the wine and simmer until the liquid has evaporated. Pour in the tomato juice and water; simmer a few minutes. Add the couscous and simmer for 10 minutes. Season with sea salt and pepper to taste, then add the oregano, lemon juice, lemon zest, and chilli pepper.

Remove the couscous from the heat and let sit, covered, for 10 minutes. Stir to break the snapper fillet into bite-sized pieces, and serve. 🍲

gnocchi di patate e porcini
potato dumplings in porcini mushroom sauce

People who say gnocchi is boring have never tasted good gnocchi. The error most people commit when making gnocchi themselves is to overwork the dough, which results in very tough dumplings. Choosing the right potatoes is also paramount for great gnocchi—the potato flavor should be prevalent and the sauce should complement, not mask, it.

For sauce:

2 tbsp/30 mL extra-virgin olive oil

2 cloves garlic, chopped

2 cups/500 mL sliced porcini mushrooms (preferably frozen) or 1½ oz (45 g) dried, reconstituted

2 cups/500 mL seeded and finely chopped tomatoes (use canned if fresh are not available)

salt and pepper

2 bunches basil

1 bunch Italian parsley, chopped

1 tbsp/15 mL butter

For gnocchi:

2 lb/1 kg potatoes, of roughly equal size

2½ cups/550 mL all-purpose (plain) flour, plus extra for dusting

1 whole egg

2 egg yolks

½ cup/125 mL grated grana padano cheese

pinch of grated nutmeg

salt and pepper

To prepare the sauce, heat the olive oil in a sauté pan over medium heat. Sauté the garlic, and just before it turns golden, add the mushrooms and sauté until the vegetables are lightly browned. Add the tomatoes, season to taste with salt and pepper, and cook until the liquid is reduced to a creamy consistency. Reduce the heat so that it's just hot enough to keep the sauce warm until ready to serve.

In the meantime, bring the unpeeled potatoes to a boil in a large pot of salted water. Reduce the heat and simmer until the potatoes are cooked, at least 4 minutes. Drain the potatoes and lay them on a table or countertop to cool. As soon as they are cool enough to touch, peel them, then press them through a potato ricer or food mill (do not use a food processor).

Spread the riced potato on a floured wooden board and sprinkle with the flour. Add the egg and egg yolks, grana padano, nutmeg, and salt and pepper to taste. Using your hands, mix the dough gently to form a ball. Cut slices about 1 inch (2.5 cm) thick, then cut each slice into strips 1 inch (2.5 cm) thick; roll to form tube shapes. Cut each tube into 1-inch (2.5 cm) dumplings. Roll each dumpling with your thumb onto the tines of a fork, leaving a thumb indentation on one side and tine marks on the other. Continue dusting the dough with flour during this whole process.

Plunge the gnocchi into a big pot of boiling salted water. As soon as they float to the surface (about 3 minutes), remove them with a slotted spoon.

Tear the basil leaves by hand into small pieces. Add the basil, parsley, and butter to the sauce. To serve, place the gnocchi in a warmed ceramic bowl and pour the sauce on top. Toss gently.

maccheroni e peperoni
macaroni in bell pepper sauce

This recipe makes me think of gardens in the late summer, when the peppers (capsicums) are firm and shiny, succulent and sweet. The aroma of roasted peppers in the kitchen takes me down memory lane—this is the dish I prepared as a teenager for my friends after a night out. We would come back to my parents' house, being careful not to wake them up, and later laugh about the fact that I always ended up with more sauce than anyone else!

Maccheroni is the Italian name for all types of macaroni, including penne and rigatoni. Use whichever you like for this dish, or even a thick spaghetti. The sauce is too heavy, though, for a fine noodle or egg noodle.

Makes 4–6 servings

3 bell peppers (capsicums), 1 each yellow, red, and orange

1 banana pepper (capsicum), chopped

6 plum (Roma) tomatoes

1 lb/500 g macaroni (your favorite type)

1/2 cup/125 mL extra-virgin olive oil

2 cloves garlic, crushed

4 anchovies, chopped

1 chilli pepper, chopped

1 medium onion, finely chopped

salt and pepper

1 bunch basil, chopped

1/2 cup/125 mL chopped Italian parsley

grated caciocavallo cheese, for garnish

Grill the bell and banana peppers (capsicums) on a hot barbecue or under the grill in the oven, turning occasionally until the entire skin is blistered and blackened. Remove the peppers (capsicums) from the heat and place in a bowl, cover with plastic wrap, and let cool. Once the peppers (capsicums) are cool, remove the skins and seeds, and rinse gently. Cut the peppers (capsicums) into diamond shapes and set aside.

Peel the tomatoes and cut them in half, then cut each half in three lengthwise. Set aside.

Cook your favorite macaroni al dente in a big pot of boiling salted water.

In the meantime, prepare the sauce. Heat the olive oil in a saucepan over medium heat. Sauté the garlic, anchovies, and chilli pepper for 1 minute. Add the onion and cook for another 5 minutes. Add the peppers (capsicums); season with salt and pepper to taste. Stir in the tomatoes. Lower the heat and simmer for about 15 minutes, stirring often to prevent sticking and adding a bit of water if necessary.

Drain the pasta and toss with the sauce, along with the basil and parsley. Cook for 1 minute. Serve topped with grated caciocavallo.

pesce / fish

involtini di branzino al finocchio
mediterranean sea bass fillet
and fennel

It's important to have a good fishmonger. Fish is highly perishable, so you need someone who not only offers good variety but also knows how to handle the fish properly. Always look for a clean store with no fishy odor. Take the time to talk to the fishmonger and get to know him or her.

When I prepare any fish I follow a few rules. The skin on large fish is usually thick and tough, so I tend to remove it. On smaller fish, if the skin is very thin, I leave it on.

Makes 4 servings

8 4-oz/115 g sea bass fillets	2 cloves garlic, crushed
4 fennel bulbs	½ tsp/1 mL crushed fennel seeds
salt and pepper	½ cup/125 mL roasted black olives, pitted
grated zest of 1 blood orange	
grated zest of 1 lemon	2 tbsp/30 mL white wine
2 tbsp/30 mL extra-virgin olive oil	½ cup/125 mL blood orange juice
	1 bunch chopped Italian parsley

Rinse the sea bass fillets under cold running water and pat dry. Carefully remove all the pin bones.

Prepare the fennel by cutting off the top of each bulb, reserving the fronds. Cut the bulbs in half, then crosswise in slices about ½ inch (5 mm) thick. Chop enough fronds to make ½ cup/125 mL.

Season the fish fillets with salt and pepper. Sprinkle with chopped fennel fronds and grated orange and lemon zest. Roll each fillet into a tight bundle and set aside.

Heat the olive oil in a frying pan. Add the garlic and fennel seeds and toast the fennel seeds for about 1 minute. Add the olives and fennel slices and sauté until a light golden color. Season to taste with salt and pepper.

Place the fish on top of the fennel, pour in the wine, and cook until the wine has evaporated. Pour in the orange juice, cover, and simmer for about 8 minutes. Adjust the seasoning to taste, stir in the parsley, and serve at once atop the remaining fennel fronds.

pesce   fish

cozze in pentola
mussels with peas and white wine

I know this recipe is a departure from my roots, but it tastes so good, I just have to share it with you. At a restaurant that I once worked at, one of the most popular dishes on the menu was mussels in a white wine and cream sauce. Then came the 1990s, and everyone became cautious about cooking with cream. Well, I say they're all crazy! Cream is still good to cook with…in moderation, of course.

Be careful with these mollusks—you might become addicted to them.

Makes 4 servings

4 lb/2 kg fresh mussels	1 cup/250 mL green peas
1 tbsp/15 mL olive oil	½ cup/125 mL diced fresh tomatoes
1 tbsp/15 mL butter	1 sprig fresh tarragon
2 cloves garlic, crushed	¼ cup/50 mL heavy cream
salt and pepper	crusty bread, for dipping
½ cup/125 mL white wine	

Scrub the mussels in cold water with a stiff brush and pull off the beards.

Heat the olive oil and butter in a saucepan over medium-high heat. Sauté the garlic for 1 minute. Add the mussels and season with salt and pepper. Stir in the wine, peas, tomato, tarragon leaves, and cream. Cover with a lid and steam until the mussels open, 3–4 minutes. Discard any mussels that do not open.

Remove the mussels with a slotted spoon and place them in a bowl.

Reduce the liquid in the pan and add salt and pepper to taste. Pour the sauce over the mussels and serve with lots of warm crusty bread for dipping.

trancia di salmone alle olive
salmon steak with roasted black olives

I always eat salmon a little undercooked, as the flesh is creamier and very pleasant. Strong yet delicate, salmon is a favorite of many customers at the restaurant. We use it as our fallback dish on busy nights when we want to make it simple for the kitchen.

This dish goes especially well with sautéed broccoli or cauliflower.

Makes 4 servings

3 tbsp/45 mL extra-virgin olive oil	salt and pepper
2 cloves garlic, crushed	4 tbsp/60 mL white wine
4 sprigs thyme	juice of 1 lemon
8 shallots, julienned	1 tbsp/15 mL grated lemon zest
½ cup/125 mL roasted black olives, pitted	1 tbsp/15 mL butter
4 8-oz/225 g salmon steaks	

Heat the olive oil in a sauté pan over medium heat. Add the garlic, thyme, and shallots and cook for 1 minute. Add the olives and simmer gently.

Season the salmon steaks with salt and pepper and place in the pan. Turn the heat to high, sear the salmon on one side, turn it over, and add the wine, lemon juice, and lemon zest. Cover and cook for about 3 minutes. Remove from the heat and add the butter, stirring it into the sauce to incorporate. Serve at once. 🍲

caciucco
seafood stew

Just about every town on the coasts of Italy has its own style of fish soup. Although at first glance they might all seem the same with their garlic and tomato, wine and bony fish, if you look closely and taste them, you'll soon realize there are subtle but obvious differences. This seafood stew is the one I learned to make in Tuscany's Versilia region. If available, use sea capon, red mullet, and conger eel instead of the monkfish, calamari, and sea bass.

Makes 4 servings

4 tbsp/60 mL extra-virgin olive oil	8 oz/225 g monkfish tail, cut in 4 pieces
4 cloves garlic, chopped	8 oz/225 g calamari, cut in short strips
1 medium onion, chopped	
2 bay leaves	8 oz/225 g sea bass or 2 fillets, cut in half
1 bunch thyme	4 jumbo shrimps
12 littleneck clams in their shells, scrubbed and rinsed	16 mussels in their shells, scrubbed and rinsed
½ cup/125 mL white wine	
2 cups/500 mL chopped fresh plum (Roma) tomatoes	1 lemon
1 cup/250 mL chicken stock	4 slices crusty bread
1 chilli pepper, chopped	crushed garlic
salt and pepper	olive oil, for garnish

Heat the olive oil in a heavy-bottomed pot over high heat. Sauté the garlic, onion, bay leaves, and thyme for 1 minute. Place the clams in the pot and pour in the wine. Cover the pot and cook the clams for a few minutes, until they open. Discard any that do not open.

Add the tomatoes, chicken stock, and chilli pepper. Season to taste with salt and pepper and simmer for 1 minute. Gently place the monkfish tail in the pot, followed by the calamari, sea bream, shrimps, and mussels. Simmer gently for about 8 minutes. Taste and adjust the seasoning. Squeeze the juice of the lemon over top.

Rub the bread slices with crushed garlic, then grill them. Spoon the stew onto the garlic toast, sprinkle olive oil on top, and enjoy.

gamberi e fagioli
sweet shrimp and cannellini beans

In the fall, just after watering season, the irrigation canals in Italy are abundant with sweet shrimp, crawfish, and smelt. Anyone can catch them easily with nothing more than a homemade net. Osterie throughout the region fry up their daily catch: a bowl of shrimp and beans with a glass of wine—you can't go wrong with that. I like to keep the shells on the shrimp for this dish, but feel free to remove them if you prefer.

Makes 4 servings

3 tbsp/45 mL extra-virgin olive oil	1½ cups/375 mL cannellini beans
2 shallots, finely minced	½ cup/125 mL chopped roasted red peppers (capsicums)
1 tsp/5 mL fennel seeds, crushed	
2 lb/1 kg pink shrimp	salt and pepper
½ cup/125 mL white wine	2 tbsp/30 mL chopped fresh chervil
1 tbsp/15 mL white wine vinegar	

Heat the olive oil in a sauté pan over medium heat. Add the shallots and fennel seeds and cook for 1 minute. Add the shrimps, wine, and vinegar; cook for 1–2 minutes.

Stir in the beans and red peppers (capsicums) and season to taste with salt and pepper. As soon as the shrimp and beans begin to sauté, cover and cook for 2 minutes. Stir in the chervil, adjust the seasoning to taste, and serve at once. 🍲

capesante con pancetta
roasted sea scallops with bacon

When buying scallops, make sure they are fresh and have not been chemically treated—befriending your fishmonger can be very beneficial! Scallops are quick and versatile to cook. They are great in pasta, as an appetizer or main course, marinated raw or cooked, fried, sautéed, or baked. Just remember, the longer you cook them, the tougher they will be.

Makes 4 servings

16 large sea scallops	2 shallots, finely chopped
16 slices flat pancetta	1 tbsp/15 mL capers
2 tbsp/30 mL extra-virgin olive oil	1 tbsp/15 mL balsamic vinegar
1 tbsp/15 mL butter	$\frac{1}{2}$ cup/125 mL red wine
1 clove garlic, lightly crushed	

Rinse the scallops and pat dry. Wrap each scallop with a slice of pancetta, leaving the top and bottom exposed.

Heat the olive oil in a heavy-bottomed pan over medium-high heat. Add the butter and the scallops, searing them until golden on the bottom. Flip the scallops and add the garlic and shallots to the pan. Cook the scallops for another minute.

Add the capers and balsamic vinegar, cooking until the vinegar has evaporated. Pour in the wine and cook for another 2 minutes. Serve at once.

storione in agrodolce
sturgeon fillet in red wine vinegar sauce

As a boy I would go fishing for sturgeon with my uncle on Italy's great Po River. Although the fishing was highly regulated, we still managed to get at least one for ourselves and some to sell.

Sturgeon is a prehistoric-looking fish; its texture is firm and similar to swordfish when cooked. Swordfish or any other firm white fish would work in this recipe.

Makes 4 servings

2 tbsp/30 mL vegetable oil	2 tbsp/30 mL red wine vinegar
2 cups/500 mL cipolline (Italian pearl onions)	4 tbsp/60 mL tomato sauce
salt and pepper	4 8-oz/225 g sturgeon steaks, each 1 inch (2.5 cm) thick
2 tbsp/30 mL sugar	2 tbsp/30 mL Italian parsley, chopped

Heat the vegetable oil in a sauté pan over medium heat. Add the cipolline, season to taste with salt and pepper, add the sugar, and cook gently until the cipolline are golden. Sprinkle the vinegar over the cipolline and cook 1–2 minutes to allow some of the vinegar's acidity to evaporate. Stir in the tomato sauce and cook until the cipolline are soft. If the pan is too dry, add a bit of water.

Rinse the sturgeon steaks under cold running water and pat dry. Place the steaks in the pan so they are surrounded by the cipolline but not covering them. Cook, covered, for about 6 minutes, shaking the pan occasionally to prevent sticking. Add the parsley and serve at once.

halibut ai funghi
halibut and chanterelle mushrooms

Halibut, a fish from the North Atlantic, was almost unknown in Italy until recently. There it's known by its English name, as very few people know its name in Italian: ippoglosso (truth be told, I had to look it up myself). Bright white, meaty, and delicate, halibut lends itself to many styles of preparation. If halibut is not available, use swordfish or any firm white fish.

Makes 4 servings

2 tbsp/30 mL light olive oil	1 tbsp/15 mL chopped fresh tarragon
4 8-oz/225 g halibut steaks	4 tbsp/60 mL white wine
salt and pepper	6 tbsp/90 mL heavy cream
1½ cups/375 mL sliced leeks, white part only	1 tbsp/15 mL butter
1½ cups/375 mL chanterelle mushrooms, cleaned, large ones halved	1 tbsp/15 mL chopped chervil
1 cup/250 mL grape tomatoes, halved	

Heat the olive oil in a heavy-bottomed pan over high heat. Season the halibut with salt and pepper and sear until slightly golden. Transfer to a plate.

Add the leeks and chanterelle mushrooms to the pan and sauté gently until the vegetables are wilted. Add the tomatoes and tarragon, then return the fish to the pan to sear the other side.

Pour in the wine and cook until it has evaporated. Pour in the cream; cover the pan to cook for about 6 minutes. Transfer the fish to a plate.

Add the butter and chervil to the sauce, stir, and adjust the seasoning to taste. Cook until the liquid is reduced to the desired consistency, about 1 minute or less. Drizzle the sauce over the fish and serve at once.

ragù di moscardini
sautéed baby octopus

My first real restaurant job was in 1975, at Trattoria dall'Amelia in Mestre, near Venice. One day, Chef shouted for me. "Clean this," he ordered. Being from the center of northern Italy, I had never seen an octopus before, let alone cleaned one. It took some time to get the hang of it, but was it ever worth it! Chef let me try some of the cooked octopus, and the flavor and texture were fantastic. It's a taste experience I've never forgotten.

If cooked properly, these tiny octopus will be crunchy but not tough. They're particularly good served over slices of grilled polenta. Sometimes I also add a few fresh or frozen peas in the last few minutes of cooking.

Makes 4 servings

½ cup/50 mL extra-virgin olive oil	2 tbsp/30 mL tomato paste
2 lb/1 kg tiny octopus, blanched	2 cups/500 mL fresh plum (Roma) tomatoes, peeled, seeded, and chopped
1 medium onion, chopped	
4 cloves garlic, chopped	salt and pepper
1 cup/250 mL white wine	

Heat the olive oil in a medium saucepan. Add the octopus and sauté until the flesh wrinkles, about 2 minutes. Some browning isn't a problem.

Add the onion and garlic, stirring to prevent burning. Add the wine and cook until it evaporates. Stir in the tomato paste and cook until dry, about 3–5 minutes. Add the tomatoes, season to taste, and simmer for 15–25 minutes, or until the octopus is fork-tender.

seppie al nero
squid stewed in its own sauce

I first tried this dish at Trattoria dall'Amelia, where I worked as a teenager. Among all the new things I was experiencing, this was the strangest. Don't let the squid's appearance turn you off—you'll be amazed at how good it tastes. Serve with polenta or a risotto, or on spaghetti.

Makes 4 servings

2 lb/1 kg squid	½ cup/125 mL finely chopped onion
3 tbsp/45 mL extra-virgin olive oil	1 chilli pepper, chopped
2 cloves garlic, finely chopped	½ cup/125 mL white wine

Clean the squid, retaining the ink sacs. Cut the squid tubes in half, then into 2-inch (5 cm) strips. Wash well and pat dry with paper towels.

Heat the olive oil in a sauté pan over medium heat. Add the garlic, onion, and chilli pepper and cook for about 1 minute. Add the squid and sauté for a few minutes, stirring well.

Over a bowl, squeeze the ink sacs to extract the ink. Stir in the wine. Strain and pour the liquid over the squid in the pan. Season to taste with salt and pepper, and cook over high heat for about 5 minutes, until the sauce is black and reduced. Serve at once.

pollame / poultry

pollo alla fiorentina
florentine fried chicken

A colleague back in Italy had the task of roasting chicken for the hotel staff twice a week. He put great effort into it, making the skin perfectly crisp and golden. He loved chicken so much that his dream was to move to America and open a restaurant-farm where he would raise, cook, and serve chicken, fried, roasted, and grilled. When I arrived in North America, I called to give him the bad news: everybody makes chicken that way here, even the chain restaurants. But move over, Southern-style fried chicken—it's time to taste the original!

Note: Dried herbs can be a substituted for fresh, but use fresh if available.

Makes 4–6 servings

4 bay leaves	3 eggs
2 cloves garlic	2 tbsp/30 mL chopped Italian parsley
1 sprig thyme	salt and pepper
1 sprig rosemary	2 cups/500 mL all-purpose (plain) flour
1 sprig sage	
juice of 2 lemons	4 cups/1 L grapeseed oil, light olive oil, or other light oil
1 yellow-skinned grain-fed chicken, weighing 2–3 lb/1–1.5 kg	

With a mortar and pestle, crush the bay leaves, garlic, thyme, rosemary, and sage to extract the flavor. Add the lemon juice, then pour the mixture into a clean plastic bag.

Quarter the chicken, remove most of the bones, and cut each quarter in half (or ask your butcher to do this). Rinse and pat dry. Put the chicken in the plastic bag with the herbs and lemon juice and refrigerate for 2–3 hours.

Beat the eggs in a bowl, add the parsley, and season with salt and pepper. Remove the chicken from the bag and dredge each piece with flour, coating well and shaking off any excess. Dip each chicken piece into the egg mixture to coat well. Dredge again with the flour.

Fry the chicken in the oil at 275°F (140°C) until golden-crisp; the oil should not be too hot or it will burn the chicken skin before it cooks the meat.

Season the chicken with salt and pepper, and enjoy.

fagiano all'uva
roasted pheasant with green grapes

When the yearly hunting season in Italy opens, the riversides are teeming with hunters looking for hares and pheasants. My uncle used to take me along. Needless to say, I didn't catch much, but my uncle was a seasoned hunter and he always brought home a variety of game.

Makes 4 servings

1 cup/250 mL seedless green grapes	1 cup/250 mL diced pancetta
½ cup/125 mL white wine	1 tbsp/15 mL wildflower honey
4 8-oz/225 g pheasant breasts, skin on	2 tbsp/30 mL verjuice or 1 tbsp/ 15 mL white wine vinegar
salt and pepper	2 cups/500 mL seedless grapes (red, green, and black in equal amounts)
2 tbsp/30 mL extra-virgin olive oil	
4 shallots, finely minced	1 tbsp/15 mL butter

Puree the 1 cup/250 mL of green grapes and ¼ cup/50 mL of the wine in a blender. Pass through a fine mesh strainer and set aside.

Season the pheasant breasts with salt and pepper. Heat the oil in a skillet over medium-high heat. Cook the pheasant, skin side down, until golden, about 4 minutes. Turn the pheasant over, add the shallots and pancetta, and cook for 2 minutes. Sprinkle on the remaining ¼ cup/50 mL wine and cook until it evaporates.

Add the grape/wine juice, honey, and verjuice or vinegar; cook for about 5 minutes over low heat. Increase the heat to medium, add the grapes, and simmer, covered, for about 5 minutes.

Transfer the pheasant to a plate and cover with tinfoil. In the meantime, reduce the sauce by about half, until it has a creamy consistency. This might take 5 or more minutes, depending on how liquid the sauce is at this point. Season to taste with salt and pepper, add the butter, and return the pheasant to the pan to reheat.

pollo alla cacciatora
chicken cacciatora

All cooks need to have a fallback traditional recipe in their repertoire—let this be it! This easy dish is one of the first I was allowed to cook on my own. For a simple meal, serve it with grilled polenta, buttered noodles, steamed rice, or mashed potatoes. Substitute porcini or chanterelle mushrooms for champignons, and you've changed the class of this dish—you will make a bella figura (good impression).

Makes 4 servings

8 chicken legs	½ cup/125 mL white wine
salt and pepper	2 red bell peppers (capsicums), cut into wedges
4 tbsp/60 mL extra-virgin olive oil	
6 cloves garlic, finely chopped	2 cups/500 mL white champignon mushrooms, quartered
1 medium onion, finely chopped	
2 stalks celery, finely chopped	1 cup/250 mL plum (Roma) tomatoes, seeded and diced
1 medium carrot, finely chopped	½ cup/125 mL chicken stock
2 bay leaves	½ bunch Italian parsley, chopped

Season the chicken legs with salt and pepper. Heat the oil in a heavy-bottomed pot over high heat. Sear the chicken legs, until golden; turn over and sear the other side. Add the garlic, onion, celery, carrot, and bay leaves to the pot; stir and let cook for about 4 minutes. Pour in the wine and cook until it evaporates.

Add the peppers (capsicums), mushrooms, tomatoes, and stock and stir well. Reduce the heat to low and simmer, covered, for about 20–30 minutes.

When the chicken is cooked, transfer it to a plate and let it sit, covered, for 10 minutes. Reduce the sauce to a creamy consistency, adjust the seasoning, and stir in the parsley. Return the chicken to the pot to reheat and serve with the sauce spooned over top.

galletto alle spèzie
spiced cornish game hen

From the time we started developing this recipe at the restaurant, we knew it was going to be a hit. The Asian spices are not overpowering, but complement the game hen. Perfect served with spinach, Brussels sprouts, bok choy, or broccoli.

Note: Use pre-ground spices or grind them yourself in a spice grinder or coffee mill.

Makes 4 servings

For marinade:	For game hens:
½ tsp/2 mL ground fennel seeds	2 Cornish game hens
½ tsp/2 mL ground coriander seeds	2 tbsp/30 mL vegetable oil
½ tsp/2 mL ground star anise	2 tbsp/30 mL butter
½ tsp/2 mL paprika	4 cloves garlic, crushed
½ tsp/2 mL ground cardamom seeds	1 sprig fresh sage
1 tsp/5 mL sugar	1 sprig rosemary
2 tbsp/30 mL vegetable oil	1 bay leaf
	salt and pepper
	2 cups/500 mL cubed boiled potatoes

Preheat the oven to 450°F (230°C).

Combine all the marinade ingredients in a small bowl. Split the Cornish game hens in half at the backbone, brush on the marinade, and marinate for at least 1–2 hours.

Heat the oil and butter in a roasting pan over medium heat. Place the marinated game hens, skin side down, in the pan and cook on top of the stove for about 10 minutes. Turn the hens over, add the garlic, herbs, salt and pepper, and potatoes, and bake in the oven for about 10 minutes, reducing the heat to 400°F (200°C) if the meat and potatoes start to brown too much.

Turn the oven off and open the door, keeping it ajar. Let the meat sit for 10 more minutes in the oven. Remove from the oven and gently remove the ribs and hip bones from the hens.

To serve, scoop the potatoes into the center of individual serving plates, along with your choice of vegetables, and place a hen half on top of each.

involtino di pollo alle melanzane
chicken rolls with eggplant

When you're feeling a little playful in the kitchen, try this recipe. Involtini—stuffed rolls of meat or fish—were very popular when I was growing up in Italy, and one never knew what they would be stuffed with. Experiment with the many possible combinations—turkey, pork, veal, beef. Fish is also a great choice for lighter meals.

Makes 4 servings

2 long (Japanese if available) eggplants	1 clove garlic, minced
4 large boneless, skinless chicken breasts	2 tbsp/30 mL finely chopped onion
	2 tbsp/30 mL capers
pepper	1 sprig thyme
extra-virgin olive oil, for dressing the eggplant	4 tbsp/60 mL white wine
1 lb/500 g smoked scamorza cheese	2 tbsp/30 mL chopped plum (Roma) tomatoes
1 tbsp/15 mL extra-virgin olive oil	1 bunch Italian parsley, finely chopped
1 tbsp/15 mL butter	

Cut the eggplants lengthwise into ½-inch (5 mm) slices. Salt and set aside to drain for up to 30 minutes, to remove bitterness.

Slice each chicken breast at a 45-degree angle into four slices. Flatten the slices with a meat mallet to an even thickness.

Dry the eggplant and season with pepper and olive oil. Grill lightly—they shouldn't be too brown. Trim the ends so they are the same length as the chicken slices.

Place a slice of eggplant on a slice of chicken breast and top with a slice of scamorza; roll up the meat. Repeat this procedure with the remaining chicken breast slices. Align four rolls and skewer them with two bamboo sticks long enough to just penetrate the meat, to keep the rolls from unraveling.

Heat the olive oil and butter in a medium skillet over medium-high heat. Sear the skewered rolls on both sides until golden. Add the garlic and onion, and cook for 2–3 minutes, until soft and translucent.

Stir in the capers and thyme leaves. Pour in the wine and cook until it evaporates. Add the tomato and simmer, covered, for 10 minutes. Sprinkle in the parsley, then transfer the chicken to individual serving plates or a serving platter.

Remove the bamboo sticks, spoon the sauce over top, and serve.

petto d'anatra con funghi chiodini
duck breast with mushrooms

Growing up on a farm is a great way to start a culinary life. My parents always had plenty of ducks and on occasion one would end up in a pot. This is a modern version of a duck stew we typically ate in the autumn, when mushrooms are plentiful.

Makes 4 servings

4 boneless young duck breasts, each weighing 8–12 oz/225–340 g	1 cup/250 mL honey mushrooms, separated, or your favorite mushroom, sliced
salt and pepper	2 cups/500 mL grape tomatoes, cut in half
4 tbsp/60 mL sherry	
1 tbsp/15 mL red wine vinegar	½ cup/125 mL chicken stock
4 cloves garlic, peeled and chopped	1 bunch Italian parsley, chopped

Rinse the duck breasts under cold running water and pat dry with paper towels. Score the skin lightly and season with salt and pepper.

Heat a large skillet over medium-high heat and cook them, skin side down, until the skin is crisp and the meat has released its fat, about 5–10 minutes.

Remove most of the fat from the skillet, reserving a spoonful, and turn the duck breasts over. Sprinkle with the sherry and vinegar and cook until the liquid evaporates. Remove the duck wrap in tinfoil, and set aside.

To the same skillet add the reserved duck fat and the garlic. Just before the garlic turns brown, add the mushrooms and season with salt and pepper. Add the tomatoes and sauté for 2–3 minutes.

Add the chicken stock and return the duck breasts to the pan. Increase the heat to high and cook the sauce for a few minutes, until it is reduced to the desired consistency. Stir in the parsley and serve.

petto di tacchino ai carciofi
turkey cutlets with minted artichokes

Turkey is not only for the holidays—it's delicious anytime, and cooking turkey cutlets is fast and easy. And don't be afraid of fresh artichokes. Choose artichokes with tight heads that feel heavy and are green or gray-green in color.

Makes 4 servings

juice of 1 lemon	1 medium white onion, finely chopped
12 small fresh globe artichokes	½ cup/50 mL white wine
2 lb/1 kg boneless turkey breast, cut into 8 cutlets of equal size	grated zest of 2 lemons
salt and pepper	½ cup/50 mL chicken stock, plus more as needed
1 tbsp/15 mL butter	2 tbsp/30 mL finely chopped Italian parsley
1 tbsp/15 mL extra-virgin olive oil	2 tbsp/30 mL chopped mint
2 cloves garlic, crushed	

Add the lemon juice to a bowl of cold water to acidulate the water. To prepare the artichokes, cut off the top quarter and discard. Remove the tough outer leaves by bending them back and snapping them off at the base. Peel the stem, if necessary. Cut the artichokes in half and remove the fuzzy centers, or chokes (small artichokes shouldn't have much of a center). Cut the artichokes into thin wedges, immediately submerging them in the acidulated cold water as you do so, to prevent discoloring.

With a meat mallet, pound the turkey breasts to ½ inch (2 cm) thick. Season with salt and pepper. Heat the butter and olive oil in a sauté pan over medium-high heat, and sear the turkey cutlets until lightly golden on one side.

Add the garlic and onion and cook for 2 minutes. Add the artichokes, wine, and lemon zest, then turn the cutlets over to cook on the other side. Once the wine has evaporated, add the chicken stock. Cook for another 2 minutes, adding more stock if the pan becomes too dry.

Transfer the turkey to a serving plate. Add the parsley and mint to the sauté pan, stirring to incorporate them, and simmer to reduce the sauce to a creamy consistency. Adjust the seasoning to taste, spoon the sauce over the cutlets, and serve. ☕

carne / meat

130

fegato alla veneziana
venetian liver and onions

If you love liver, this recipe just might become one of your favorites. The thin slices of liver and the sweetness of the onion go hand in hand. Enjoy this dish with polenta or mashed potatoes.

Makes 4 servings

1 lb/500 g calf's liver	3 cups/750 mL thinly sliced sweet white onion
salt and pepper	½ cup/125 mL white wine
2 tbsp/30 mL extra-virgin olive oil, plus more for seasoning	½ cup/125 mL Italian parsley
2 tbsp/30 mL butter	½ lemon

Trim the hard sinew and outer membrane from the liver, being careful not to crush it. Slice the liver into scaloppine about 2 inches (5 cm) wide and ½ inch (1 cm) thick; season with olive oil, salt, and pepper.

Heat 2 tbsp/30 mL of olive oil and the butter in a skillet over medium-low heat. Gently sauté the onion until it is caramelized. Turn the heat to high and immediately add the liver. Sear on both sides. Pour in the wine and cook until it evaporates. Season to taste with salt and pepper, parsley, and a squeeze of lemon juice, and stir well. Serve at once.

manzo brasato aromatico
braised short ribs in red wine

Maybe it's because I grew up in the interior of northern Italy, where good fish is not as plentiful as elsewhere in the country, but I am very comfortable cooking meats. Whether they're boiled, stewed, or thinly sliced and grilled with Asian seasonings, short ribs are one cut of meat I'm particularly fond of. This recipe is wonderful accompanied by lightly sautéed bok choy, spinach, or potatoes.

Makes 4–6 servings

1 sprig each rosemary, thyme, and sage	salt and pepper
1 tsp/5 mL fresh ginger, chopped	3 cloves garlic, crushed
3 star anise	1½ cups/375 mL diced onion
3 bay leaves	1 cup/250 mL diced carrots
2 tbsp/30 mL extra-virgin olive oil	½ cup/125 mL diced celery
1 tsp/5 mL butter	4 tbsp/60 mL tomato paste
4 lb/2 kg beef chuck short ribs, frenched (ask your butcher)	1 cup/250 mL red wine
	3 cups/750 mL unsalted beef stock

To prepare the herb sachet, place the rosemary, thyme, sage, ginger, star anise, and bay leaves onto a 4x4-inch (10x10 cm) square of cheesecloth, gather the cloth into a bundle, and tie it up with twine.

Heat the oil and butter in a heavy-bottomed pot over medium-high heat. Season the short ribs with salt and pepper and sear until the meat is golden brown. Add the garlic, onion, carrot, and celery, and stir until the vegetables are translucent. Stir in the tomato paste and cook for 2–3 minutes. Add the herb sachet.

Pour in the red wine and boil until it evaporates. Pour in the stock, reduce the heat to low, and simmer, covered, for at least 2½ hours, or until the meat is fork-tender. Remove the meat from the pot, wrap in tinfoil, and set aside.

Reduce the sauce to a creamy consistency, strain out all the vegetables, and season to taste with salt and pepper. Return the meat to the pot with the sauce and reheat to serve. ☺

costine di maiale e verze
pork spareribs and cabbage

Spareribs are a favorite for summer barbecues. This recipe captures the style of the ribs I ate growing up—few things work as well together as pork and cabbage. This hearty dish is especially good in winter, served with potato salad or grilled polenta.

Makes 4 servings

4 whole racks baby back ribs	2 tbsp/30 mL red wine vinegar
salt and pepper	1 tbsp/15 mL tomato paste
1 tbsp/15 mL sugar	1 cup/250 mL chopped fresh tomatoes
3 tbsp/45 mL extra-virgin olive oil	
2 cloves garlic, crushed	1 cup/250 mL chicken stock
1 cup/250 mL julienned onion	1 head cabbage, hard outer leaves removed
½ cup/125 mL white wine	

Wash the ribs and pat dry. Cut between each bone to separate them, and season with salt, pepper, and sugar.

Heat the olive oil in a heavy-bottomed pot over medium-high heat. Add the ribs and sear until golden brown. Add the garlic and onion and cook for a few minutes. Pour in the wine and vinegar and cook until they evaporate. Stir in the tomato paste and then the tomatoes. Pour in the chicken stock, reduce the heat, and simmer for about 20 minutes, covered.

In the meantime, remove each leaf from the cabbage and cut out the center spine, splitting the leaf in two. Cut the cabbage into wide juliennes. Add the cabbage to the meat, season with salt and pepper, stir, and cover. Simmer until the cabbage is tender, about 10 minutes.

coda di bue al barolo
barolo-braised oxtail

When I was growing up in Italy, my mother often prepared oxtail, as it was an affordable meat. Back in those days we thought of braising— which requires robust cuts of meat—as a bad thing. How things have changed! Today braised meats have achieved gourmet status. This dish is excellent with mashed potatoes or polenta of any type, or break the meat down, remove the bones, and use it for pasta, gnocchi, or risotto. A good wine will enhance the flavor of this dish, so don't skimp.

Makes 4 servings

1 sprig each rosemary, sage, thyme, and parsley, for sachet (or $\frac{1}{2}$ tsp/ 2 mL of each if using dried herbs)

2 tbsp/30 mL extra-virgin olive oil

1 tbsp/15 mL butter

4 lb/2 kg oxtail

salt and pepper

4 cloves garlic

1 cup/250 mL diced onion

1 cup/250 mL diced celery

1 cup/250 mL diced carrots

1 cup/250 mL peeled, diced parsnips

4 bay leaves

4 tbsp/60 mL tomato paste

2 cups/500 mL Barolo wine

4 cups/1 L unsalted beef stock

To prepare the fresh herb sachet, place the herbs on a 4x4-inch (10x10 cm) square of cheesecloth, gather the cloth into a bundle, and tie it up with twine. (If you are using dried herbs, they can simply be added loose.)

Heat the oil and the butter in a heavy-bottomed pot over medium-high heat. Season the oxtail with salt and pepper and sear until golden brown on all sides. Add the garlic, onion, celery, carrots, parsnip, and bay leaves, and stir until the vegetables are translucent. Stir in the tomato paste and cook for a few minutes. Toss in the herbs.

Pour in the wine and boil until it evaporates. Pour in the beef stock and simmer over low heat, covered, for at least 1 ½ hours; when the meat falls off the bone easily, it's done. Transfer the meat to a plate and cover. Allow it to cool completely before touching it again.

Pass the vegetables through a food mill or blend in a food processor and return to the pot with the juices. Reduce the sauce to the desired thickness and season to taste with salt and pepper. Return the meat to the pot and reheat to serve.

coniglio in umido
rabbit in apricot sauce

Rabbit is a very popular meat in Italy and, being low in fat, one of the healthiest. My parents used to keep rabbits by the hundreds. We sold them, and on occasion one would end up in a pot—delicious!

Note: Marinate the apricots in the grappa 8–12 hours ahead of time.

Makes 4–6 servings

1 cup/250 mL dried apricots, halved	2 bay leaves
4 tbsp/60 mL grappa di moscato	$\frac{1}{2}$ cup/125 mL white wine
2 small rabbits, approximately 3 lb/ 1.5 kg each, deboned and cut into large pieces (ask your butcher)	2 tbsp/30 mL tomato paste
	4 plum (Roma) tomatoes, peeled, seeded, and quartered
salt and pepper	2 cups/500 mL chicken stock
4 tbsp/60 mL vegetable oil	1 tsp/5 mL chopped chives
16 shallots, sliced	2 tbsp/30 mL chopped fresh sorrel
3 star anise	

Marinate the dried apricots in the grappa (see note).

Season the rabbit pieces with salt and pepper. Heat the oil in a sauté pan and cook the rabbit until golden. Stir in the shallots and grappa-soaked apricots and cook for 1 minute. Add the star anise, bay leaves, and wine; cook until the wine evaporates. Stir in the tomato paste and cook for 2–3 minutes.

Add the tomatoes and chicken stock and simmer gently, covered, for at least 1 hour. Test a rabbit leg for doneness by pressing gently on the thickest part—the meat should give and break apart easily. Remove the rabbit and set aside, covered with tinfoil.

Reduce the pan juices to a creamy consistency, season to taste with salt and pepper, and add the chives and sorrel, stirring to mix well. Return the rabbit to the pan with any juices it may have purged while cooling, to reheat.

To serve, arrange the rabbit pieces on a plate with the shallots, apricots, and tomatoes around them and the sauce poured over top.

costine di agnello glassate al balsamico
balsamic-glazed lamb ribs

If you are lucky enough to find lamb ribs, grab them and run home to try this recipe.

This dish has become so popular at Mistura that I can't even suggest taking it off the menu without creating an uproar.

Makes 4 servings

2 tbsp/30 mL extra-virgin olive oil

4 lb/2 kg lamb ribs

salt and pepper

5 cloves garlic, crushed

2 onions, diced

2 carrots, diced

1 stalk celery, diced

8 sprigs rosemary

8 sprigs thyme

2 bay leaves

1 cup/250 mL red wine

2 cups/500 mL chicken stock

½ cup/125 mL tomato paste

tzatziki sauce, for serving

For glaze:

1 cup/250 mL balsamic vinegar

¼ cup/75 mL maple syrup

2 tbsp/30 mL tomato paste

Heat 1 tbsp/15 mL olive oil in a large skillet or casserole dish over medium-high heat. Season the ribs with salt and pepper and sear in batches until browned on both sides. Remove from the pan and set aside.

Lower the heat to medium and add the remaining 1 tbsp/15 mL oil. Sauté the garlic, onion, carrots, celery, rosemary, thyme, and bay leaves until the vegetables are soft and golden brown, about 5 minutes. Add the wine and cook until it evaporates. Return the lamb to the pan and add the chicken stock and tomato paste. Cover and cook for 1½ hours, or until the lamb is tender. Remove the lamb from the pan and keep warm.

Preheat the oven to 350°F (180°C).

To prepare the glaze, strain the pan juices into a bowl, discarding any solids. Pour into a sauté pan along with the balsamic vinegar, maple syrup, and tomato paste. Bring to a boil and cook until thick and syrupy. Brush the glaze over the ribs and reheat in the oven for 10 minutes, or until heated through. Serve with tzatziki sauce on the side.

braciola di maiale con salvia e limone
pan-seared pork chops with lemon sage

The sweet aroma of pan-fried pork chops is mouth-watering, and the meat marries naturally with sage and lemon. The acidity of the lemon cuts the fat and freshens the flavor—the main reason why Italian dishes, from grilled meat to fish to pasta, are often served with fresh lemon. Just remember, a drop of lemon juice goes a long way.

If you are considering leaving out the cream, don't. Even though it is only a small amount, it imparts a flavor that completes the dish.

Makes 4 servings

2 lemons	1 tbsp/15 mL butter
4 pork chops	1 bunch sage
all-purpose (plain) flour, for dredging	4 shallots, finely minced
salt and pepper	½ tsp/2 mL Dijon mustard
1 tsp/5 mL vegetable oil	2 tbsp/30 mL heavy cream

Zest the lemons. Peel and separate one of them into segments. Juice the second lemon.

Lightly dredge the pork chops with flour seasoned with salt and pepper. Heat the vegetable oil and 1 tsp/5 mL butter in a skillet over medium-high heat. Add the chops and sear on both sides until golden. Transfer to a plate.

Melt the remaining 2 tsp/10 mL butter in the pan. Add the sage leaves and cook until they release an aroma. Add the shallots and cook for 1 minute. Add the lemon zest, return the chops to the pan, and sprinkle them with the lemon juice. Stir in the lemon segments and Dijon mustard and cook for a few minutes.

Pour in the cream and simmer until the pork chops are cooked and the sauce is well reduced. Season to taste with salt and pepper.

crocchette di rosa
rosa's veal-and-rice croquettes

Working in a restaurant means I'm often busy six or seven days a week.
Fortunately, my wife, Rosa, has the strength to rise to the challenge.
She has quite a few recipes in her arsenal, and this one is a favorite.
When I come home late at night, often after midnight, it's a welcome
surprise to find a plate of these croquettes waiting for me on the table.
Rosa has learned, though, not to leave too many—for my own good!

Makes 4–6 servings

For croquettes:

4 cups/1 L cooked risotto or
leftover rice

2 cups/500 mL lean ground veal

2 eggs

½ cup/125 mL grated Parmigiano-
Reggiano cheese

½ cup/125 mL Italian parsley,
chopped

1 tbsp/15 mL extra-virgin olive oil

1 tbsp/15 mL butter

2 cloves garlic, chopped

½ cup/150 mL finely diced onion

½ cup/150 mL finely diced celery

½ cup/150 mL finely diced carrot

1 cup/250 mL green peas

salt and pepper

For breading:

2 eggs

1 cup/250 mL milk

2 tbsp/30 mL grated Parmigiano-
Reggiano cheese

salt and pepper

2–3 cups/500–750 mL breadcrumbs,
as needed

light olive oil, for frying

In a mixing bowl, combine the rice, ground veal, eggs, Parmigiano,
and parsley.

Heat the oil and butter in a skillet over medium heat and sauté the garlic,
onion, celery, carrot, and peas until the vegetables are translucent.

Add the vegetables to the rice and meat, mixing well. Using your hands, form into log-shaped croquettes 2½ inches (6 cm) long and 1 inch (2.5 cm) thick. Pack them well so that they will not fall apart during cooking.

To prepare the breading, beat the eggs with the milk and Parmigiano; season with salt and pepper. Spread the breadcrumbs on a plate or tray. Gently dip the croquettes in the egg wash, then roll in the breadcrumbs.

Pan-fry the croquettes in light olive oil or bake at 375°F (190°C), turning occasionally, until they are crisp and the veal is well cooked, at least 10 minutes.

legumi / vegetables

finocchi alla milanese
milanese fennel cutlets

I have yet to meet anybody who doesn't enjoy breaded meat, fish, or vegetables. Perhaps it's the richness of the frying that makes us like them so much. But I have a different take on it—if you use the right ingredients and treat them with respect, the result will be hard to resist. To me, fennel tastes so good that frying it is merely the final step in preparing a great little treat. If the frying oil is kept hot, the fennel won't be greasy.

Makes 4–6 servings

2 fennel bulbs	salt and pepper
2 eggs	3 cups/750 mL fresh breadcrumbs
½ cup/125 mL milk	½ cup/125 mL grated grana padano cheese
2 tbsp/30 mL Italian parsley, finely chopped	extra-virgin olive oil, for frying
1 tsp/5 mL fresh thyme	1 tbsp/15 mL butter

Bring a pot of salted water to a boil. Remove the stringy inedible outer leaf from each fennel bulb, clean the bottom, and cut the bulb lengthwise into wedges. Plunge the fennel into the boiling water for 30 seconds. Drain and cool on paper towels.

In a bowl, combine the eggs, milk, parsley, and thyme; season to taste with salt and pepper. Add the fennel wedges and gently stir to coat.

On a tray, mix together the breadcrumbs and the grana padano. Coat each fennel wedge by pressing it firmly into the breadcrumb mixture, being careful not to crush the fennel by pressing too hard.

In a frying pan over medium-high heat, pour olive oil to about ½ inch (5 mm) deep—there should be just enough so the fennel won't burn to the bottom of the pan, but it shouldn't be submerged in the oil—and add the butter. When it has melted, arrange the fennel wedges so they fit comfortably in the pan; they should be neither too tight against each other nor too loose. Fry the fennel until golden, turning as necessary so that it colors evenly. Remove from the oil with a slotted spoon and drain on paper towels. Serve hot or at room temperature.

cardi al forno con pecorino
baked cardoons with pecorino

The cardoon, a sweet vegetable resembling white celery, is a close cousin of the artichoke. Although cardoons (young Scotch thistles) can be relatively difficult to find, they're well worth seeking out. Like artichokes, they must be handled with care, as they tend to discolor quickly. In many locales the best season for cardoons is winter.

Makes 4–6 servings

2 bunches cardoons	2 tbsp/30 mL Italian parsley
4 slices white bread	3 tbsp/45 mL extra-virgin olive oil
4 anchovies	1 tbsp/15 mL butter, for baking dish
4 cloves garlic	2 cups/500 mL milk
½ cup/125 mL pecorino toscano cheese	salt and pepper

Preheat oven to 375°F (190°C).

Bring a pot of salted water to a boil. Separate the cardoon stalks and rinse thoroughly under cold running water. Remove the tough, stringy outer ribs by peeling the cardoons as though they were potatoes. Cut the remaining stalks into 3-inch (7.5 cm) pieces and plunge into the boiling water. Once the water has returned to a boil, remove the cardoons. Drain and cool on paper towels.

Pulse the bread, anchovies, garlic, pecorino, parsley, and olive oil in a food processor until combined.

Place the cardoons in a buttered baking dish, lining them up tightly. Pour in the milk, season with salt and pepper, and bake for 20 minutes, or until the cardoons are soft.

Sprinkle the bread mixture on top and put the dish under the grill for 1–2 minutes, just until the topping is golden-crisp.

carote carmellate al limone
caramelized lemon carrots

Growing up in the country has its rewards. My home garden was always ready to give up seasonal delicacies, and carrots were one of them. I only had to scout the patch for the biggest fronds to pull up a tasty treat.

I recommend using small bunched carrots or a variety of heirloom carrots rather than large, thick carrots for this recipe. They can be cut or left whole, as I have done here.

Makes 4–6 servings

3 bunches carrots (approximately 20)	2 tbsp/30 mL lemon juice
1 tbsp/15 mL extra-virgin olive oil	1 cup/250 mL water
salt and pepper	1 tbsp/15 mL grated lemon zest
2 tbsp/30 mL honey	2 tbsp/30 mL Italian parsley

Wash and peel the carrots, leaving some of the green tops on.

Heat the olive oil in a sauté pan over medium heat. Add the carrots and season to taste with salt and pepper. Add the honey, lemon juice, and water; simmer until all the water has evaporated and the carrots are cooked. At this point the pan should be dry and the carrots will begin to caramelize. Let them brown, being careful not to let them burn. Add the lemon zest and parsley and toss to mix.

rapini con le acciughe
sautéed rapini with anchovies

"Eat it, it's good for you"—so my mother used to say when she served rapini (also known as rabe, rape, and canola). As with other bitter vegetables, I wasn't too crazy about rapini, but my tastes have since changed and now I love it. My clientele does too, and rapini will always be on the menu in one dish or another. The most popular is pasta with rapini and a generous grating of pecorino cheese.

I got the idea to add cream at a restaurant in Bari, where this is a traditional dish. The chef there told me that cream helps take away the rapini's bitterness by adding a mild sweetness.

Makes 4–6 servings

2 bunches rapini	1 red chilli pepper, chopped
4 tbsp/60 mL extra-virgin olive oil	salt and pepper
4 cloves garlic, crushed	½ cup/125 mL water
8 anchovy fillets, chopped	4 tbsp/60 mL heavy cream (optional)

Rinse the rapini under cold running water. Cut away the bottom 2 inches (5 cm) of the stems and discard. Chop the remaining rapini into 2-inch (5 cm) pieces.

Heat the olive oil in a skillet, add the garlic and sauté for 1 minute. Add the anchovies and chilli pepper, and cook until the anchovies have almost disintegrated. Add the rapini and season with a pinch of salt (just a pinch—the anchovies are already salty) and pepper. Pour in the water and cover with a tight-fitting lid. Cook the rapini for about 10 minutes, until soft, making sure it doesn't dry out too much.

If you wish, add the cream at the end of the cooking, once the other liquid has been absorbed or evaporated, and cook just long enough for the rapini to absorb the cream.

piselli al prosciutto e scalogno
fresh green peas with prosciutto and shallots

I remember as though it were yesterday being a young boy and having to eat green peas—the tough, discolored skin, a tasteless ingredient in a tough veal stew. I would pick each one out, hiding them in my pocket or throwing them around the room, angering my keepers. Of course, I am talking not about my parents but of summer camp. In retrospect, those were fun times—and I got over my hang-up about peas.

Makes 4–6 servings

5 slices prosciutto di Parma, about 4 oz/155 g in total	3 cups/750 mL fresh (or frozen) shelled green peas
1 tbsp/15 mL extra-virgin olive oil	1/2 cup/125 mL vegetable stock
2 tbsp/30 mL butter	salt and pepper
1 cup/250 mL finely sliced shallots	1 sprig mint, finely sliced

Chop the prosciutto into a fine julienne no longer than 1 inch (2.5 cm).

Heat the oil and butter in a sauté pan over medium heat. Add the prosciutto and sauté for 1–2 minutes. Stir in the shallots and cook for another minute. Add the peas and vegetable stock. Season to taste with salt and pepper, and cook until the peas are tender—about 5 minutes for fresh, 3 minutes for frozen. Stir in the mint and serve.

cavoletti alle pancetta e mandorle
brussels sprouts with pancetta and almonds

Many people avoid Brussels sprouts. Maybe the sulfurous odor turns them off, or maybe they have only ever eaten them overcooked, which gives the sprouts a bitter taste, or undercooked, and tasting too green. When cooked properly, Brussels sprouts are wonderful, and I love them. I think you will too, after you've tried this recipe.

Makes 4–6 servings

1 lb/500 g Brussels sprouts, halved	$\frac{1}{2}$ cup/125 mL chopped pancetta
1 tsp/5 mL vegetable oil	$\frac{1}{2}$ cup/125 mL skinless almonds
2 tbsp/30 mL butter	salt and pepper
2 cloves garlic, crushed	1 cup/250 mL water
2 shallots, finely minced	

Blanch the Brussels sprouts in a pot of boiling salted water for 2 minutes. Drain and cool on paper towels.

In the meantime, heat the oil and butter in a sauté pan over medium heat and sauté the garlic and shallots for 1 minute. Add the pancetta.

Crush the almonds slightly with a mallet to bring out the flavor and add them to the pan; sauté for about 1 minute. Add the Brussels sprouts, season to taste with salt and pepper, and pour in the water. Simmer until all the water has evaporated and the sprouts are cooked. Be careful not to overcook them or they will be mushy.

fagiolini in salsa
green beans in savory vinaigrette

French beans are very thin green beans, often sold prepackaged. Although they cost a bit more than regular green beans, the taste is worth it. They are sometimes available in yellow (often known as wax beans), which also work well in this recipe.

This dish is best enjoyed at room temperature—perfect for summertime.

Makes 4–6 servings

1 lb/500 g French beans, or regular green beans if not available

4 tbsp/60 mL extra-virgin olive oil

1 clove garlic, minced

2 tbsp/30 mL minced shallots

2 tbsp/30 mL red wine vinegar

2 tbsp/30 mL tomato sauce

salt and pepper

2 tbsp/30 mL finely sliced basil

Boil the beans in salted water until they are done to your liking, and cool in ice water.

Heat 1 tbsp/15 mL olive oil in a skillet over medium heat. Add the garlic and shallots and cook until soft and translucent. Sprinkle the vinegar on top and cook until it evaporates. Immediately add the tomato sauce, season to taste with salt and pepper, and simmer for 1 minute. Stir in the basil and remove from heat. Set aside to cool.

Once the dressing has cooled, pour it over the beans, tossing to mix well.

funghi al pomodoro
sautéed mushrooms with tomato sauce

One of the many good reasons to go for a walk in the woods is the pleasure of finding mushrooms. Of course, you or your companion must know which mushrooms to pick. Many times my father and I returned home from our walks with large amounts of mushrooms and big grins on our faces.

Makes 4–6 servings

1 cup/250 mL whole shiitake mushrooms	4 cloves garlic, crushed
1 cup/250 mL oyster or king oyster mushrooms	4 shallots, thinly sliced
	1 bay leaf
1 cup/250 mL whole honey mushrooms	1 tsp/5 mL oregano
	½ cup/125 mL chicken stock
1 cup/250 mL whole chanterelle mushrooms	½ cup/125 mL tomato puree
6 tbsp/90 mL extra-virgin olive oil	salt and pepper

Remove the stems from the shiitake mushrooms. Cut the oyster or king oyster mushrooms into strips and remove the hard parts of the stems. Separate the honey mushrooms. Clean the stems of the chanterelle mushrooms, rinse them with cold water, and dry thoroughly.

Heat the olive oil in a heavy-bottomed frying pan over high heat. Add the garlic, shallots, bay leaf, and oregano; sauté for 3–4 seconds. Before the vegetables become too golden, add the mushrooms and sauté for a few more seconds. Pour in the chicken stock and cook until the broth is absorbed or evaporates.

Add the tomato puree and season to taste with salt and pepper. Cook for 2 more minutes.

peperonata veneta
sautéed peppers

At the end of the summer, local markets are flooded with peppers (capsicums). These beautiful-tasting vegetables can be preserved easily by first roasting them and then either freezing or canning them. But before you do that, make yourself some peperonata—sautéed peppers. Use them as a hot garnish for roasted chicken or at room temperature as an antipasto or topping for bruschetta.

Makes 4–6 servings

3 red bell peppers (capsicums)

2 yellow bell peppers (capsicums)

1 green bell pepper (capsicum)

2 medium onions

¼ cup/50 mL extra-virgin olive oil

4 cloves garlic, sliced

8 plum (Roma) tomatoes, peeled and seeded

salt and pepper

3 tbsp/45 mL red wine vinegar

1 bunch basil, coarsely chopped

1 bunch Italian parsley, coarsely chopped

Preheat the oven to 475°F (245°C). Roast the peppers (capsicums) under the grill, turning occasionally, until the skins are entirely blistered and blackened. Remove from the oven and place in a bowl. Cover the bowl with plastic wrap and set aside until cool. Once the bell peppers (capsicums) are cool, remove the skins and seeds, rinse gently, and cut the bell peppers (capsicums) into wedges. Set aside.

Remove the first layer from the onions and cut them into wedges (about 8 wedges per onion). Heat the olive oil in a medium saucepan. Sauté the onions and garlic lightly for 1–2 minutes. Add the bell peppers (capsicums) and tomatoes. Stir well and simmer, covered, for about 30 minutes, stirring occasionally to prevent sticking.

Season to taste with salt and pepper and add the vinegar. Cook for another 5 minutes, covered. Just before you turn off the heat under the pan, stir in the basil and parsley.

castagne e legumi arrosto
caramelized chestnuts and winter vegetables

I use fresh chestnuts as much as possible when they are available. In this recipe they are complemented by naturally sweet vegetables. This is definitely a winter vegetable dish, and the sweetness of the vegetables and the flavor combinations are sure to make it a favorite in your repertoire. I like to sprinkle good balsamic vinegar on top and sometimes add a chopped pear or apple to the mix. It is wonderful as an accompaniment to turkey, capon, lamb, or wild game.

Makes 4–6 servings

2 tbsp/30 mL butter

2 tbsp/30 mL extra-virgin olive oil

2 medium carrots, cut into small sticks

1 cup/250 mL cipolline (Italian pearl onions), peeled and blanched

4 cloves garlic, chopped

4 slices buttercup squash (pumpkin), peeled

1 fennel bulb, sliced into 4 pieces

2 cups/500 mL fresh chestnuts, peeled and blanched, or vacuum-packed chestnuts

salt and pepper

Heat the butter and olive oil in a heavy-bottomed pan over medium-low heat. Add the carrots and cipolline and sauté for 3–4 minutes. Add the garlic, squash (pumpkin), fennel, and chestnuts. Season to taste with salt and pepper and cook until tender, turning the vegetables over gently when one side has turned golden. Maintain the medium-low heat throughout the cooking process to allow the vegetables to caramelize without burning.

Note: If you prefer, bake the vegetables in a 375°F (190°C) oven for about 15–20 minutes, or until soft and golden.

gratin di verdure
vegetarian shepherd's pie

I created this dish for the hit TV series Restaurant Makeover, and I still get e-mails asking me for the recipe. It's a vegetarian reworking of the traditional shepherd's pie; if you omit the cheese, it will be sure to please any vegan guest at your dinner table.

Makes 8 servings

2 tbsp/30 mL extra-virgin olive oil	½ cup/125 mL canned chickpeas, drained
4 cloves garlic, crushed	salt and pepper
1 cup/250 mL julienned onion	1 tsp/5mL Cajun spice mix, or to taste
2 cups/500 mL white cabbage, shredded	½ cup/125 mL green peas
½ cup/125 mL julienned carrots	½ cup/125 mL corn
1 cup/250 mL small cauliflower florets	2½ cups/625 mL mashed potato
1 cup/250 mL diced tomatoes	1 cup/250 mL grated grana padano cheese

Preheat the oven to 375°F (190°C).

Heat the olive oil in a frying pan over high heat. Add the garlic, onion, cabbage, carrot, cauliflower, tomatoes, and chickpeas. Season to taste with salt, pepper, and Cajun spice. Cook for 2–3 minutes—you want to cook the vegetables quickly but not to overcook them. Place the vegetables in a casserole dish and spread them out evenly.

Combine the peas and corn and spread on top of the vegetables. Spread the mashed potato to cover the vegetables and top with the grana padano. Bake for 30 minutes or until the top is crisp.

dolci / sweets

frittelle di carnevale
carnival donuts

Who doesn't love carnival? From Venice to New Orleans to Rio de Janeiro, this festive season is celebrated with parties and good eats, donuts among them. Enjoy these fried treats on their own or filled with zabaglione (see page 188).

Makes 40 small donuts

½ cup/125 mL brandy	1½ cups/300 mL all-purpose (plain) flour, sifted
1 cup/250 mL raisins	4 large eggs
2 tbsp/30 mL sugar	
¼ tsp/2 mL salt	1 tsp/5 mL vanilla extract
¼ cup/50 mL butter	sunflower oil, for frying
1 cup/250 mL water	powdered sugar, for dusting

Pour the brandy over the raisins to moisten them. Set aside.

In a pot, combine the sugar, salt, butter, and water, and bring to a boil. Add the flour and beat with a wooden spoon. Turn the heat down to medium and cook until the dough forms a ball and comes away from the sides of the pot. Remove from the heat.

Add the vanilla extract and then the eggs, one by one, mixing well, until little bubbles form in the dough. Stir in the raisins. Scoop up the dough with a wet teaspoon to form small freeform donuts.

Pour sunflower oil into a deep, heavy-bottomed frying pan to about 1 inch (2.5 cm) deep and heat to 350°F (180°C). Put in as many donuts as will fit loosely, and fry until they are a deep golden color. Remove from the oil with a slotted spoon or skimmer and drain on paper towels. Continue deep-frying the donuts until all the dough is used up.

Once they are cool, dust the donuts with powdered sugar. 🍲

torta sabbiosa
lombardy sand cake

In my childhood home, weekends were awaited with anticipation. My mother spent all day Saturday preparing the pasta, meats, and desserts for Sunday lunch. This cake was always on the table, ready to be offered to visitors, and with luck we would have some left over for ourselves.

I like to serve this cake with fragole al balsamico and whipped cream on the side.

Makes 12 servings

1 cup/250 mL all-purpose (plain) flour	1 tbsp/15 mL good-quality vanilla extract
1 cup/250 mL potato starch	grated zest of 1 lemon
1 tsp/5 mL baking soda	grated zest of 1 orange
¼ tsp/1 mL baking powder	2 tbsp/30 mL orange liqueur
1½ cups/375 mL butter, at room temperature	4 eggs, separated
2½ cups/550 mL sugar	1 whole egg
	powdered sugar, for dusting

Preheat the oven to 350°F (180°C).

In a medium bowl, sift together the flour, potato starch, baking soda, and baking powder.

Whip the butter with the sugar and vanilla extract to a creamy consistency. Stir in the lemon and orange zest and the liqueur. Add the egg yolks and whole egg, one by one, mixing well. Gradually add the flour mixture, mixing well to incorporate.

Whip the egg whites until soft peaks form. Gently fold into the batter, working with a spatula from the bottom of the bowl to the top, until well incorporated.

Butter and flour a 10- or 12-inch (25 or 30 cm) springform pan. Pour in the cake batter and level with a spatula or the back of a spoon. Bake for about 1 hour, or until a toothpick inserted in the center comes out clean. Do not open the oven door for the first 40 minutes of baking.

Remove the cake from the oven and allow to cool completely before turning out of the pan. Dust the cake with powdered sugar before serving.

coppa al caffè
coffee parfait

Trattoria dall'Amelia had one dessert that was always on my danger list: coffee parfait. I often saw Chef check the numbers after I had been in the walk-in fridge.

This parfait is a quick dessert to prepare for a large group of people. Long, slender glasses are ideal serving dishes, as they show off the attractive layers of the parfait. If you don't have stemware, get creative—use glass bowls or ice cream coupes, or whatever you have on hand.

Makes 4 servings

5 egg yolks	2 tsp/10 mL instant coffee powder
¼ cup/75 mL sugar	1 cup/250 mL chocolate sauce
4 tbsp/60 mL coffee liqueur	dark chocolate, for garnish
1 lb/500 g good-quality mascarpone cheese	

Place a medium bowl in a large, shallow pan of hot water. Put the egg yolks in the bowl and whip in the sugar and coffee liqueur until the mixture is pale and very thick. When lifted out with the beater, the batter should fall back onto the surface in a ribbon and sit for a few seconds before sinking back in. This process will cook the egg yolks. Set aside to cool.

Add the mascarpone and coffee powder to the eggs. Using an electric beater, whip until stiff peaks form. Be careful not to over-whip the cheese, or it will separate.

Pour a layer of chocolate sauce into a serving glass, add a scoop of the cheese mixture, another layer of chocolate, and another scoop of cheese. Continue layering until the glass is full; there should be at least five layers. Fill all the serving glasses this way and refrigerate for at least 1 hour.

Top with shavings of dark chocolate.

pere al balsamico con caprino al miele

balsamic roasted pears with whipped goat cheese

A common sight in Cremona's fruit markets is baked fruit and vegetables—from pears to apples to beetroots—making it easy for home cooks to prepare all sorts of dishes. For me, nothing finishes a great meal better than roasted fruit.

Makes 4 servings

2 tbsp/30 mL unsalted butter

4 firm, ripe Bosc pears, halved lengthwise and cored

3 tbsp/45 mL balsamic vinegar

4 oz/115 g creamy goat cheese, at room temperature

5 tbsp/75 mL wildflower honey

¼ tsp/2 mL freshly cracked black pepper

Preheat the oven to 450°F (230°C).

Melt the butter in an 8-inch (20 cm) glass baking dish on the middle rack of the oven, for about 3 minutes.

Arrange the pears, cut side down, in the butter, and roast until tender, about 20 minutes. Pour the vinegar over the pears and roast for 5 more minutes. Transfer the pears to serving plates, cut side up.

In a metal bowl, whip the goat cheese and 1 tbsp/15 mL honey with an electric mixer or beater until fluffy. Using a warm spoon, place a dollop of cheese in the center of each pear half. Drizzle the baking juices over the pears.

Top the pears and cheese with the remaining 4 tbsp/60 mL honey and freshly cracked black pepper.

torta di mele di maddalena
maddalena's apple cake

My sister-in-law, an excellent cook, often bakes a cake "just in case we have visitors"—a good plan, except that the cake is gobbled up before she has a chance to serve it to any guests. My kids and my wife love this moist cake, and this is my take on it. The apricot jelly glaze will give the cake a nice shine.

Makes 12 servings

2 lb/1 kg green or sour baking apples (approximately 6 apples)	1 tbsp/15 mL vanilla extract
juice of 2 lemons	1 tbsp/15 mL grated lemon zest
1½ cups/425 mL all-purpose (plain) flour	3 eggs
2 tsp/10 mL baking powder (or packaged Italian yeast if available)	2 tbsp/30 mL milk, plus more as needed
pinch of salt	2 tbsp/30 mL melted butter
½ cup/150 mL butter, at room temperature	3 tbsp/45 mL apricot jelly
½ cup/175 mL sugar	2 tbsp/30 mL water
	powdered sugar, for garnish

Preheat the oven to 350°F (180°C).

Peel, core, and quarter the apples. Cut each quarter in half so that each apple yields eight wedges. Sprinkle with the lemon juice to prevent discoloring, and set aside.

In a medium bowl, sift the flour, baking powder, and salt.

In a metal bowl, cream the butter with the sugar, vanilla extract, and lemon zest, using an electric mixer. Add the eggs one at a time, whipping until the batter is light and fluffy. Turn the mixer to slow and add about half of the flour mixture and 1 tbsp/15 mL milk. Mix well, then add the rest of the flour mixture. If the batter is too thick, add more milk—it should be fluffy, not runny.

Pour the batter into a greased 10- or 12-inch (25 or 30 cm) springform cake pan and level with a spatula or the back of a spoon. Arrange the apple wedges on top in a pattern, leaving about $\frac{1}{4}$ inch (1 cm) around the sides to allow for the batter to expand. Brush the apples with the melted butter. Bake for 45–50 minutes, or until a toothpick inserted in the center comes out clean. Remove the cake from the oven and let cool for 10–15 minutes before turning out onto a cake rack to cool completely.

In a saucepan over medium-low heat, dissolve the apricot jelly in the water. Brush over the top of the cooled cake. Finish the cake by dusting powdered sugar around the edges.

biscuit del dondeo
chestnut and chocolate semifreddo

Dondeo is a famous pastry shop in Cremona. It opened in 1926, and my grandfather used to sell milk, eggs, and fruit to it. Among its many high-quality pastries and famous cappuccino, its chestnut and chocolate semifreddo stands out; it has been part of our family celebrations for as long as I can remember. This is my version.

Makes 12 servings

5 eggs, separated

1 cup/250 mL sugar

1½ cups/375 mL whipping cream

½ cup/175 mL marrons glacé (candied chestnuts), chopped

½ cup/125 mL good-quality chocolate shavings

1 lb/500 g store-bought meringue

2 tbsp/30 mL powdered sugar

Place a medium bowl in a large, shallow pan of hot water, and whisk together the egg yolks and ¼ cup/50 mL sugar in the bowl until thick and fluffy. Lay plastic wrap directly on top of the mixture and refrigerate until cold.

Whip the cream and gently fold it into the egg mixture. Beat the egg whites until soft peaks form. Gradually beat in the remaining ½ cup/175 mL sugar until stiff, glossy peaks form. Gently fold into the egg yolk mixture. Fold in the chestnuts and chocolate shavings.

Crumble half of the meringue into the bottom of a 10-inch (25 cm) cake mold, pour in the batter, and crumble the remaining meringue on top, pressing down gently to even out the filling. Wrap with plastic wrap and place in the freezer for at least 6 hours.

Remove from the cake mold and sprinkle with powdered sugar to finish.

risotto al cioccolato
chocolate risotto

This may seem strange at first, but—trust me!—everyone loves it.
Chocolate risotto is a luscious version of chocolate rice pudding.
It's the perfect end to a meal that doesn't contain too much starch.

Makes 4 servings

2 tbsp/30 mL unsalted butter	1 cup/250 mL milk
1 cup/250 mL vialone nano or other risotto rice, unwashed	½ cup/125 mL heavy cream
1 vanilla bean, split	½ cup/75 mL white sugar
2 tbsp/30 mL rum	1 tsp/5 mL grated orange zest
2 cups/500 mL water	1 tsp/5 mL grated lemon zest
	½ lb/125 g dark chocolate, chopped

Melt the butter in a saucepan over very high heat. Add the rice and stir
continuously until the rice is very hot but not browned. Add the vanilla
bean, rum, and water; cook until almost all the liquid has evaporated.

Add a small amount of the milk and stir until it has been absorbed by
the rice. Continue to add the milk in small amounts until it has all been
absorbed and the rice is cooked. This process will take 15–18 minutes
in total.

Remove the pan from the heat and add the cream, sugar, orange and
lemon zest, and chocolate. Stir well to incorporate all the ingredients.
Serve at once.

dolci

tortino di frutta di bosco
mixed berry pudding

This is one recipe that really kicks. I originally wanted a cake that had apple chunks in it and was very moist, almost wet. I fiddled around and eventually came up with this—out with the apple and in with the berries!

This pudding bakes best in individual molds, so a large muffin pan is ideal to use. If you don't have one, use a ring mold or Bundt pan.

Makes 6–8 servings

butter, for greasing the mold	¼ tsp/2 mL baking soda
flour, for dusting the mold	¼ tsp/1 mL salt
½ cup/125 mL vegetable oil	½ cup/125 mL diced strawberries
1 cup/250 mL sugar	½ cup/125 mL blueberries
¼ tsp/2 mL vanilla extract	½ cup/125 mL raspberries
1 egg	
1 cup/250 mL all-purpose (plain) flour	

Preheat the oven to 350°F (180°C).

Generously butter and flour the cups of a large muffin tin (or use paper liners) or a 10-inch (25 cm) ring mold or Bundt pan. This is an important step, as the batter is very sticky.

Combine the oil and sugar, stirring until they have a creamy consistency. Add the vanilla extract and egg, and mix well.

In a medium bowl, combine the flour, baking soda, and salt. Fold in the creamed sugar mixture. Add the strawberries and then the blueberries. Stir in the raspberries very gently. Pour the batter into the baking dish and bake for 50 minutes, if using a cake pan, or 10–15 minutes, if using a muffin tin. A toothpick inserted in the center of the cake should come out dry. ☕

latte fritto al limoncello
fried milk bites with limoncello

Fried milk is perhaps more Spanish than Italian, but it is becoming increasingly popular on the dessert menus of Italian restaurants. This version is made with Limoncello, a lemon liqueur made in the south of Italy. When I started making this dessert at Mistura, I had no idea how it would be received, but so many of my customers like it, it's been on the menu for years.

Makes 8 servings

For lemon cream:

2 cups/500 mL milk

6 tbsp/90 mL sugar

grated zest of 2 lemons

1 tsp/5 mL vanilla extract

6 tbsp/90 mL all-purpose (plain) flour

3 tbsp/45 mL cornstarch (cornflour)

6 tbsp/90 mL Limoncello liqueur

juice of 1 lemon

4 egg yolks

For frying:

sunflower oil, for frying

2 tbsp/30 mL granulated sugar, or as needed

2 eggs

flour, for dredging

To prepare the lemon cream, boil 1½ cups/375 mL milk in a saucepan with the sugar, half of the lemon zest, and the vanilla extract.

In a bowl, combine the flour with the cornstarch (cornflour). Add the remaining ½ cup/125 mL milk, Limoncello, lemon juice, and egg yolks. Pour in the scalded milk, mixing well and quickly so that no lumps form and the consistency is creamy.

Pour the mixture back into the pan and boil until it becomes solid, just a few minutes. Immediately spread the mixture to about ½ inch (2 cm) thick on a tray lined with waxed paper. Cool completely, for as long as 8–12 hours if possible. When it is ready, cut the cooled cream into diamond shapes.

Pour sunflower oil into a deep, heavy-bottomed frying pan to about 1 inch (2.5 cm) deep and heat to 350°F (180°C).

In the meantime, mix the sugar with the remaining lemon zest. Beat the eggs in a bowl. Dredge the lemon cream diamonds with flour on a plate, shake off any excess, and dip them in the beaten eggs, coating well. Again dredge the diamonds with the flour, shake well to remove any excess, and fry in the oil until crisp and golden.

Drain the fried cream on paper towels for a few seconds, then roll in the lemon sugar and transfer to a plate. Serve the diamonds warm on their own or with fruit compote.

zabaglione classico
classic zabaglione

This is by far the simplest dessert to prepare, and so versatile. Serve as a side dish with panettone, stollen, or kugelhopf. Add some berries if you wish to lighten the flavor. Or let the zabaglione cool, fold in meringue and whipped cream, and freeze to make a semifreddo. Many more recipes come to mind, but really the easiest way to enjoy it is just as it is. Add a couple of cookies on the side and you're done.

Makes 4 servings

4 egg yolks

4 tbsp/60 mL sugar

½ cup/125 mL Marsala

1 tbsp/15 mL cocoa powder

In a metal bowl, beat the egg yolks with the sugar until the yolks are pale. Add the Marsala and mix well.

In the bottom of a double boiler, bring water to just below the boiling point (boiling water will make the eggs taste burned). Add the egg mixture to the top and whip for 2–3 minutes, until stiff peaks form.

Serve dusted with cocoa powder.

In a metal bowl, beat the egg yolks with the sugar until the yolks are pale. Add the Marsala and mix well.

In the bottom of a double boiler, bring water to just below the boiling point (boiling water will make the eggs taste burned). Add the egg mixture to the top and whip for 2–3 minutes, until stiff peaks form.

Serve dusted with cocoa powder.

index

Picture Credits

All color food photographs are by Christopher Campbell unless otherwise noted.

Photographs on pages 8, 13, 25, 34, 40, 54, 60, 68, 73, 80, 84, 87, 98, 103, 116, 129, 134, 140, 143, 146, 152, 173 by Andrew Capra
Photographs on pages 19, 57, 111, 164, 182 by Ian Garlick
Photograph on page 21 used with the kind permission of Nella Cutlery

Excel 2007

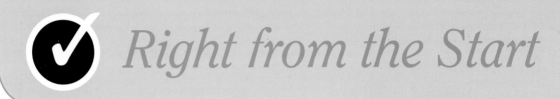

✓ *Right from the Start*

R. Chasemore

www.harcourt.co.uk

✓ Free online support
✓ Useful weblinks
✓ 24 hour online ordering

01865 888070

PAYNE-GALLWAY

Payne-Gallway is an imprint of Harcourt Education Limited, a company incorporated in England and Wales, having its registered office: Halley Court, Jordan Hill, Oxford OX2 8EJ. Registered company number: 3099304

www.harcourt.co.uk

Text © F R Heathcote 2007

First published 2007

12 11 10 09 08 07
10 9 8 7 6 5 4 3 2 1

British Library Cataloguing in Publication Data is available from the British Library on request.

ISBN 978 1 905292 37 0

Edited by John Giles
Typeset by Sparks, Oxford – www.sparks.co.uk
Cover design by Peter Stratton
Cover photo/illustration ©iStockPhotos/WaD
Printed in China by South China Printing Co. Ltd.

Acknowledgements

The author and publisher would like to thank the following individuals and organisations for permission to reproduce screenshots:

Microsoft product screenshots reprinted with permission from Microsoft

Every effort has been made to contact copyright holders of material reproduced in this book. Any omissions will be rectified in subsequent printings if notice is given to the publishers.

Websites

The websites used in this book were correct and up-to-date at the time of publication. It is essential for tutors to preview each website before using it in class so as to ensure that the URL is still accurate, relevant and appropriate. We suggest that tutors bookmark useful websites and consider enabling students to access them through the school/college intranet.

Ordering Information
Payne-Gallway, FREEPOST (OF1771),
PO Box 381, Oxford OX2 8BR
Tel: 01865 888070
Fax: 01865 314029
Email: orders@payne-gallway.co.uk

Contents

Chapter 1 – What is a Spreadsheet?

Getting started

A spreadsheet is a very useful piece of computer software, mainly used for working with numbers. Spreadsheets are used in thousands of different situations which involve doing calculations or drawing charts and are often used for planning budgets and working with financial data. Different figures can be entered and the effect of these changes will be calculated automatically.

Microsoft Excel is one of many different spreadsheet packages. In Excel, **spreadsheets** are referred to as **workbooks**. Just to make it even more confusing, a workbook can contain several **worksheets**.

In this chapter you will learn how to move around a worksheet and enter text and numbers.

 Load **Microsoft Excel**. You can do this in one of two ways:

 Either double click the **Excel** icon on your windows desktop

Figure 1.1

 Or click **Start** at the bottom left of the screen, click **Programs**, then click Microsoft Office and Microsoft Excel 2007.

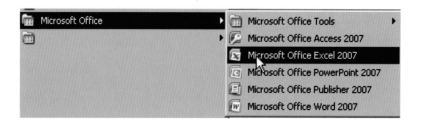

Figure 1.2

Your screen will look like Figure 1.3:

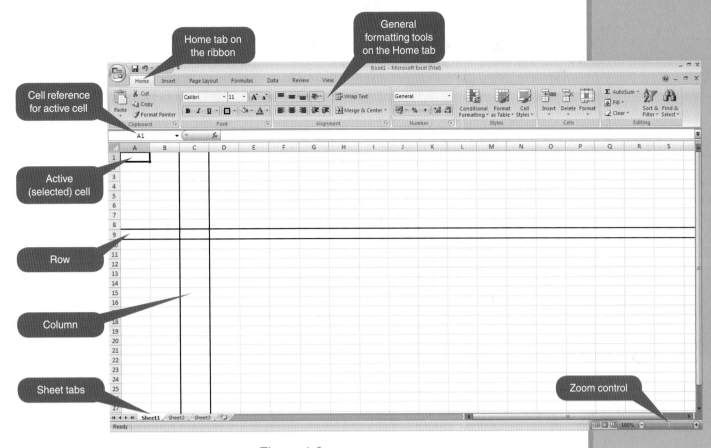

Labels on figure:
- Home tab on the ribbon
- General formatting tools on the Home tab
- Cell reference for active cell
- Active (selected) cell
- Row
- Column
- Sheet tabs
- Zoom control

Figure 1.3

▶ A worksheet contains 16,385 **columns** (referenced as XFD) and 1,048,576 **rows** which is a huge increase over previous versions of Excel. When using Excel, you can only see a few of these on the screen at a time.

▶ The columns are labelled **A**, **B**, **C** and so on. The rows are labelled **1**, **2**, **3** etc.

▶ The worksheet is divided into cells in which you can type a number, a label or a formula. The address of the cell in the top left-hand corner is **A1**, because it is in column **A** and row **1**.

▶ A **workbook** contains several blank **worksheets** named **Sheet1**, **Sheet2**, **Sheet3** etc; the sheets can be renamed to represent their purpose more closely. The maximum number of worksheets in a single workbook is 1024.

Moving around the worksheet

When you open a new workbook, cell **A1** is highlighted, showing that it is the **active cell**. When you start typing, the letters or numbers will appear in this cell.

You can move around the spreadsheet to make a cell active in any of these ways:

▶ Move the pointer using the mouse and click the left mouse button in the cell you want.

▶ Use one of the cursor or arrow keys on the keyboard to go up, down, left or right.

▶ Use the scroll bars to move over the worksheet and click the mouse to select a cell in a new location.

▶ Use the **Page Up** or **Page Down** keys.

▶ Press the **Tab** key.

Experiment!

▶ Try moving around the spreadsheet using the arrow keys, scroll bars and **Page Up** and **Page Down** keys.

▶ Try holding down the **Ctrl** key while you use any of the arrow keys. What happens?

▶ What is the name (i.e. address or cell reference) of the very last cell in the worksheet?

▶ Try typing the cell reference directly into the sheet and press **Enter** (see Figure 1.3 for where to type this).

The Zoom tool

You can easily change the size of the spreadsheet on your screen.

▶ Look at Figure 1.3; towards the bottom of the screen you can see the **Zoom** control which allows you to select different screen resolutions in a number of different ways, perhaps the most convenient being to drag the central shield shaped pointer to the left to zoom out or to the right to zoom in.

The Ribbon

As shown in Figure 1.3, the **Ribbon** is found at the top of the screen. The controls and tools which you will use are divided among a number of **tabs** which are selected by clicking on their name, for example **Home**, **Insert**, **Page Layout**, etc. Within each tab the tools and controls are collected into 'groups' of similar function, for example those to do with the control of the size and shape of fonts are collected into the **Font** group on the **Home** tab.

The Quick Access Toolbar

You can augment the standard controls on this toolbar with buttons which you find you use frequently. The default appearance of the **Quick Access Toolbar** is:

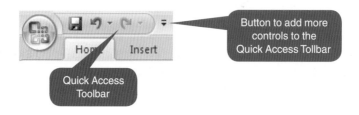

Figure 1.4

Click the **Customize Quick Access Toolbar** button and select **More Commands** from the drop-down menu. The following dialogue box opens:

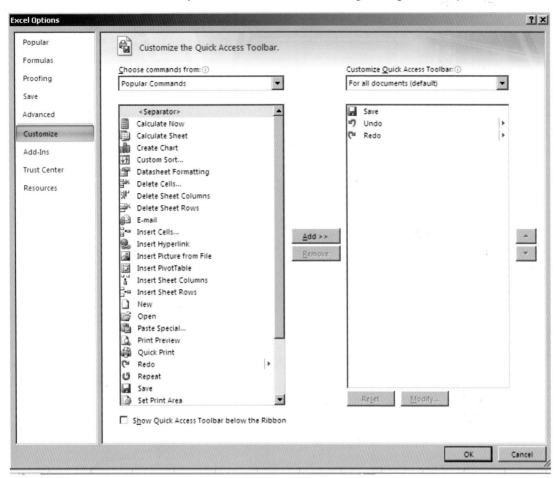

Figure 1.5

 Click the icon for the command which you want to install on the **Quick Access Toolbar** and then click the central **Add** button. When you click **OK**, the new command will be found on the **Quick Access Toolbar**. In the above example, the **Insert Sheet Rows** button is being inserted. With some experimentation, it is possible to customise the toolbar to suit your needs, although it is probably best to leave this until you are more certain about what these needs are likely to be.

Using the Help function

If at any time you aren't sure how to do something in **Excel**, you can search the **Help** files for instructions on your chosen subject. For example, let's search for help on **copying and pasting**.

 Press the keyboard shortcut **F1** (top, towards the left-hand side of your keyboard). The following **Help** dialogue box opens:

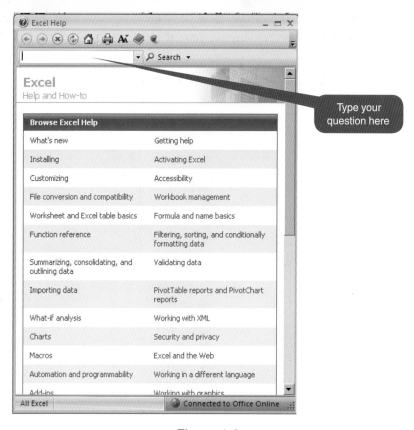

Figure 1.6

Type **Copy and Paste** into the question box and press the **Search** button or the **Enter** key. The following items of possible interest are offered:

Figure 1.7

▶ Select by clicking on **Move or copy cells and cell contents**. More options offering solutions and methods of working are offered and you can select the detailed help relevant to the work you are doing.

▶ Click the **Close** icon to close the **Help** window.

Entering data

Suppose that you have to produce a list of all the employees in an office along with the number of days of holiday they have taken so far this year.

The list will look like this:

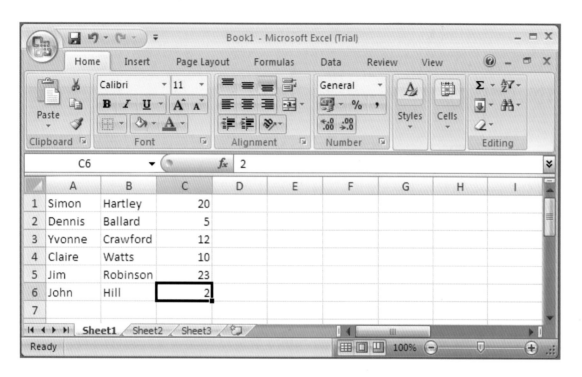

Figure 1.8

▶ Click in cell **A1**.

▶ Type the name **Simon**.

▶ Press the right arrow key.

▶ Type the surname **Hartley**. Press the right arrow key again and type the number **20** in cell **C1**.

▶ Press **Enter**, click in cell **A2** (or use the arrow keys to go there).

▶ Copy the rest of the list. If you make any mistakes, don't worry because you can correct them in a minute.

Tip:
It is often useful to keep the **Help** file visible while you are carrying out its instructions. To do this click the **Keep on top** button (shown in Figure 1.7).

Tip:
If you start to type another name beginning with, for example, **S**, in cell **A7**, Excel will guess that you are going to type **Simon** again and enter the letters for you. If you were going to type **Simon**, you can just **tab** out of the cell or press **Enter**. If you were going to type **Stuart** or some other name beginning with **S**, just carry on typing. Try it out.

Editing data

One name has been spelt wrongly. It should be spelt Clare, not Claire. There are several ways of putting it right.

First way

▶ Click in the cell containing the name Claire. You will see that the name appears in the **formula** bar, as shown below.

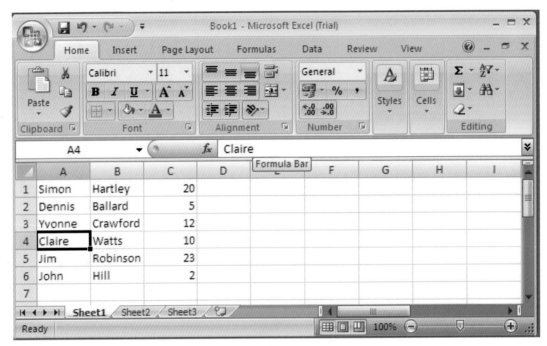

Figure 1.9

▶ Click in the **formula** bar. Use the arrow keys to move the insertion point between **i** and **r**, and then press the **Backspace** key. You will see that the change is made in the cell **A3** at the same time as you edit the name in the **formula** bar.

▶ Press **Enter** to register the change.

Second way

Another way to edit a cell is simply to type over the text in the cell. Suppose **Simon's** surname is actually **Hemmings**, not **Hartley**.

▶ Click in the cell containing the surname **Hartley**.

▶ Type **Hemmings**.

▶ Press **Enter**.

Deleting the contents of a cell

To delete the contents of a cell, click in the cell and then press the **Delete** key.

▶ Delete the surname **Robinson**.

Inserting and deleting rows and columns

We can delete the whole of row **5** so that no gap is left between **Clare**'s and **John**'s records.

▶ Right click the row header for row **5** (see Figure 1.10).

▶ Left click **Delete** from the shortcut menu which appears.

The entry for **John** moves up to row **5**.

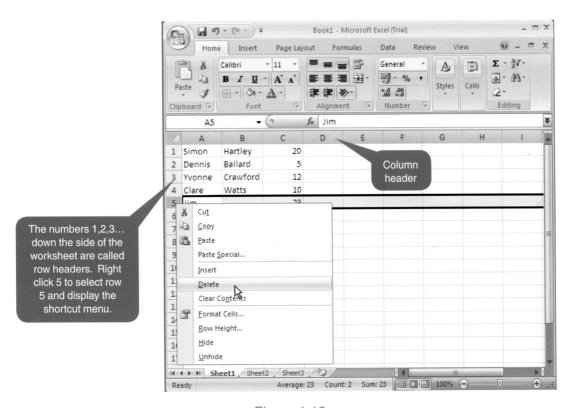

Figure 1.10

Now suppose we want to put a heading at the top of the worksheet, above the names. We need to insert a new row.

▶ Right click the row header for row **1**.

▶ Select **Insert** from the shortcut menu.

▶ Click the left mouse button in the new cell **A1**, which starts the new row.

▶ Type **Holiday Days Taken** in cell **A1**. Press **Enter**.

▶ Insert another blank line below the header in the same way (Figure 1.11).

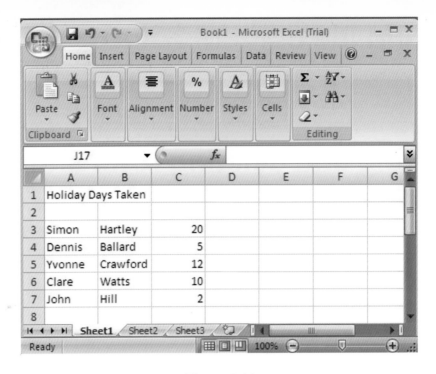

Figure 1.11

Saving your work

▶ Click the Office Button (see Figure 1.12) and click **Save As** and then select **Excel Workbook**.

Figure 1.12

▶ The **Save As** dialogue box appears (see Figure 1.13). Excel offers the default filename **Book1** for your workbook; the name appears in the **File name** box.

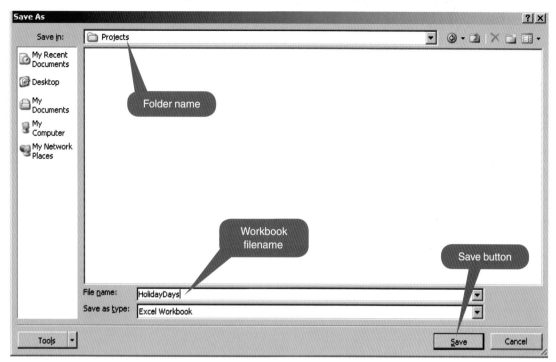

Figure 1.13

▶ Make sure the right folder is displayed in the **Save in** box, then enter the name **HolidayDays** in the **File name** box.

▶ Click the **Save** button to save the workbook.

▶ Close the workbook by selecting **Close** from the **Office Button**.

▶ Close **Excel** by clicking the close icon (the cross shape) in the top right of the window (see Figure 1.14).

Figure 1.14

Chapter 2 – Formulas

The really useful part of spreadsheets is formulas. Using a formula will enable Excel to perform calculations for you automatically.

To see how formulas work in Excel, we'll start by doing a page of 'sums'. We'll be using the following mathematical symbols:

+	add
–	subtract
*	multiply
/	divide
()	brackets are used whenever necessary

The first task is to set out the page just how you want it.

Project: Create a worksheet to do calculations

	A	B	C	D	E	F	G
1	ADD		SUBTRACT		DIVIDE		MULTIPLY
2	100.00		100.00		230.00		57.30
3	400.00		56.00		14.50		12.50
4							

Figure 2.1

▶ Open up **Excel**; a new blank workbook should automatically be created.

▶ Type the text **ADD**, **SUBTRACT**, **DIVIDE** and **MULTIPLY** in cells **A1**, **C1**, **E1** and **G1** as shown in Figure 2.1.

▶ Type all the numbers as shown in the correct cells.

Tip:
If a new workbook doesn't appear when you open Excel, just click the **Office** button and then select **New** and **Blank Workbook**.

Selecting cells

In order to format the text in certain cells by making it bold or changing the font, the cells first have to be **selected**. Try the following ways to select a range of cells:

▶ Click in the intersection of the row and column headers to select every cell in the worksheet. All the selected cells appear highlighted.

▶ Click in column header **A** to select column **A**. When you make a new selection, the previously selected cells cease to be selected (only the new selection is highlighted).

▶ Click in row header **1** to select row **1**.

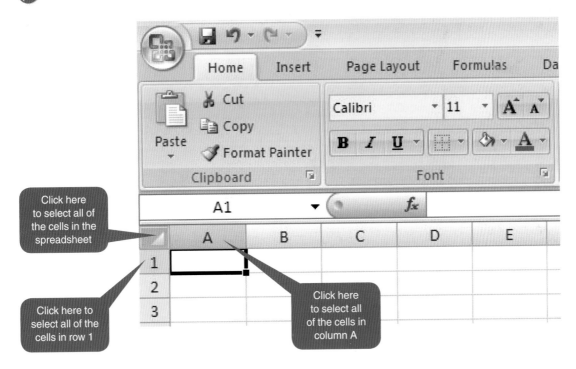

Figure 2.2

▶ Drag the mouse across cells **A1** to **G1** to select those cells.

▶ To select just cells **A1**, **C1**, E1 and **G1**, click in cell **A1** and then hold down the **Ctrl** key while you click each of the other cells.

Making text bold

You can format text in a worksheet in a very similar way to how you would within **Microsoft Word**.

▶ Make sure cells **A1** to **G1** are selected.

▶ Press the **Bold** button on the **Font** group on the **Home tab** toolbar.

Inserting a border

Cells **A4**, **C4**, **E4** and **G4** need a thick top and bottom border.

▶ Click In cell **A4**. Hold down **Ctrl** while you click each of the other cells to select them.

▶ In the **Home** tab, click the **Borders** button in the **Font** group. None of the options in the shortcut menu gives the required border, so click on the bottom option, **More borders**.

▶ A dialogue box should appear. Click the **Border** tab.

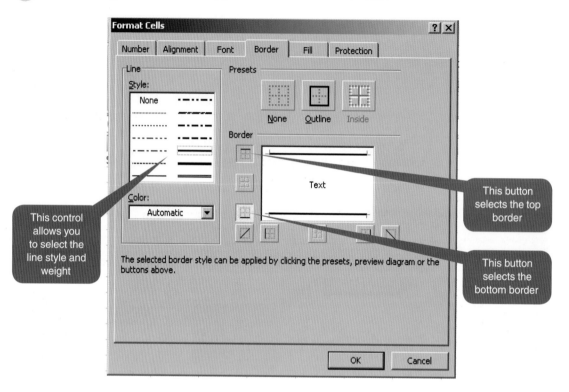

Figure 2.3

▶ Select the line style by clicking a thick line in the **Style** box; do this first.

▶ Click the **Border** boxes as shown in Figure 2.3 to specify top and bottom boxes.

▶ Click **OK**.

▶ Click in a cell away from the cells and you will see that all the cells you selected now have a top and bottom border.

	A	B	C	D	E	F	G	H
1	ADD		SUBTRACT		DIVIDE		MULTIPLY	
2	100.00		100.00		230.00		57.30	
3	400.00		56.00		14.50		12.50	
4								
5								
6								

Figure 2.4

Before you do any more work, save the workbook, naming it **Sums**.

Save button

Home   Insert

Figure 2.5

Tip:
You don't need to click **File**, **Save** – you can just click the **Save** icon on the **Quick Access Toolbar**.

Entering formulas

Formulas are entered using cell references.

▷ Click in cell **A4**.

▷ Type an equals sign = to tell Excel that you are about to enter a formula.

▷ Type **a2+a3** so that the formula appears as shown in Figure 2.6 (while you are typing you may notice that Excel tries to be helpful and offers a number of mathematical functions; just ignore these).

	SUM	▼	✕ ✓ *fx*	=a2+a3		
	A	B	C	D	E	F	G
1	ADD		SUBTRACT		DIVIDE		MULTIPLY
2	100.00		100.00		230.00		57.30
3	400.00		56.00		14.50		12.50
4	=a2+a3						
5							

Figure 2.6

▷ Press **Enter**. The answer appears!

▷ In cell **C4**, type **=c2-c3** and press **Enter**.

▷ In cell **E4**, type **=e2/e3** and press **Enter**.

▷ In cell **G4**, type **=g2*g3** and press **Enter**.

Tip:
Don't forget to type the equals = sign!

Now your worksheet should look like this:

	A	B	C	D	E	F	G	H
1	ADD		SUBTRACT		DIVIDE		MULTIPLY	
2	100.00		100.00		230.00		57.30	
3	400.00		56.00		14.50		12.50	
4	500.00		44.00		15.86207		716.25	
5								

Figure 2.7

17

Automatic recalculation

The great thing about a spreadsheet is that once you have entered the formula, you can change the contents of the other cells and the answers will still be right.

▶ Change cell **A2** to **75**. What is the answer now?

▶ Delete the contents of cells **C2** and **C3** by selecting them and then pressing the **Delete** key. What is the answer in cell **C4**?

Standard error values

If you try and make Excel do a formula it can't, an error value will appear instead of an answer.

For example, let's try and divide a number by zero:

▶ Replace the contents of the cell **E3** with **0** and click **Enter**. Now Excel will try and divide **230** by **0** – the answer when you divide anything by zero is **infinity**, which isn't a number. What answer does Excel give?

Tip:
You can undo your last action by pressing the **Undo Typing** button found on the **Quick Access Toolbar**.

Figure 2.8

	A	B	C	D	E	F	G	H
1	ADD		SUBTRACT		DIVIDE		MULTIPLY	
2	100.00		100.00		230.00		57.30	
3	400.00		56.00		0.00		12.50	
4	500.00		44.00	◊	#DIV/0!		716.25	
5								

Figure 2.9

▶ Whenever Excel returns **#DIV/0!** as the answer to a formula, it is because it is trying to divide something by zero.

▶ Delete the contents of cell **G2** by selecting it and pressing the **Delete** key. Enter a space in the cell by pressing the **Space** bar then press **Enter**. The cell is empty, but an error message has appeared in cell **G4**.

▶ If you ask Excel to do a calculation on a non-numeric value, it will give the error message **#VALUE!**.

Tip:
A space is a text (non-numeric) character even though it is invisible! Other text characters such as the letters abc would have the same effect.

	A	B	C	D	E	F	G	H
1	ADD		SUBTRACT		DIVIDE		MULTIPLY	
2	100.00		100.00		230.00			
3	400.00		56.00		0.00		12.50	
4	500.00		44.00		#DIV/0!	◇	#VALUE!	
5								
6								

Figure 2.10

Entering formulas by pointing

Instead of typing in a formula such as =a2+a3 you can use the mouse to point to the cells in the formula.

▷ Restore the worksheet to how it looks in Figure 2.9. Remember, you can use the **Undo Typing** button on the **Quick Access Toolbar** for this. Delete all the formulas in row **4**.

▷ In cell **A4**, type = and then click the mouse in cell **A2**.

▷ Type + and then click the mouse in cell **A3**.

▷ Press **Enter**. Try entering the other formulas in the same way.

▷ When you have finished experimenting, save your workbook.

Formatting cells

It is sometimes neater to have a comma to indicate thousands. For example, '1,532,000' is easier to read and grasp than '1532000'.

We'll format the cells in this spreadsheet to do this.

▷ Click in cell **A2** and drag across to cell **G3**. Right click in the selection and select **Format Cells** from the drop-down list that appears.

▷ Click the **Number** tab in the **Format Cells** dialogue box. Select **Number** from the left-hand list, and click the check box for **Use 1000 Separator (,)**.

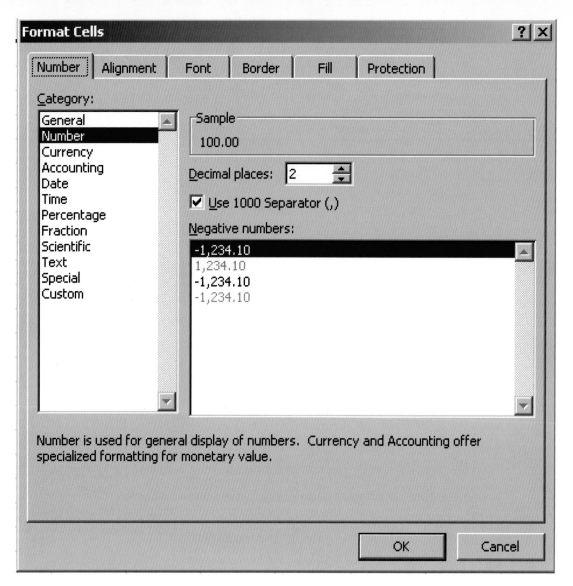

Figure 2.11

 Click **OK**. Try entering a value greater than **1000** to see how it is displayed.

 Save and close the **Sums** workbook.

Chapter 3 – Columns of Data

In this chapter we'll look at changing the way the numbers are displayed in the spread-sheet, and make Excel automatically create column totals.

Project: Create a spreadsheet to hold data on baby statistics

We will create a spreadsheet to hold data about the weights and lengths of newly born babies in a maternity ward.

▶ Open a new Excel workbook.

▶ Type the title **BABY STATISTICS** in cell **A1**. It will overflow the cell, but that's OK. Press **Enter**.

▶ Select cell **A1** again and make the text bold by clicking the **Bold** button.

▶ Now add the title **SOMERVILLE WARD** in cell **D1**. Make it **Bold** too. ——————— **B**

Changing column widths

You can change the width of column **A** so the title **Baby Statistics** fits into cell **A1**.

▶ Position the pointer so that it is on the line between column headers **A** and **B**. The pointer will change to a double-headed arrow.

Figure 3.1

▶ Press the left mouse button and hold it down while you drag to the right. The column will widen. Make it wide enough to contain the whole title.

▶ Now type the rest of the column headings as shown in Figure 3.2.

Now try a second way of widening a column.

▶ Position the pointer between the column headers of columns **D** and **E** containing the words **Somerville Ward**.

● Double click the left mouse button. The column automatically widens to fit the heading.

● Save your workbook, calling it **Stats**.

Formatting numbers

● Now fill in the rest of the headings, names and numbers.

Stats						
	A	B	C	D	E	F
1	BABY STATISTICS			SOMERVILLE WARD		
2						
3	Name	Weight (kg)	Length (cm)			
4	Anthony Goddard	3.5	50			
5	Timothy Salter	3	47.5			
6	Kerry Meridith	4.1	52.9			
7	Deborah Roberts	2.9	48.8			
8	Omar Iqbal	4	52			
9	Victoria King	3.3	51.6			
10						
11	TOTAL					
12						
13	AVERAGE					
14						
15	MAXIMUM					
16						
17	MINIMUM					
18						
19	COUNT					

Birth Stats / Daily Weights / **Sheet4**

Figure 3.2

Notice that data starting with a letter is automatically **left-justified** in a cell. **Numeric** data on the other hand is automatically **right-justified**.

The measurements would look much better if they were all shown to **2** decimal places. At the moment, if a measurement is entered as **3.0**, Excel automatically shortens this to **3**.

  Select cells **B4** to **C19** by dragging the mouse across them.

  Click the **Increase Decimal** button in the **Number** group on the **Home** tab on the **Ribbon**.

All the measurements should now be shown to **2** decimal places, as shown in Figure 3.3.

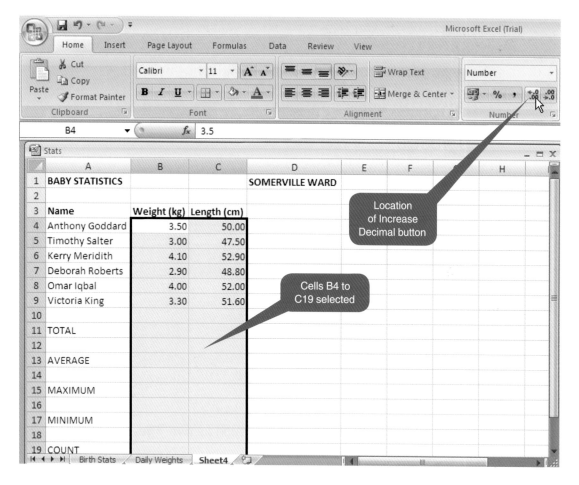

Figure 3.3

Adding a column of numbers

We want to add up the weight of each baby to get the total weight of all the babies on the ward.

 Click in cell **B11** to make it the active cell.

 Click the **AutoSum** button in the **Function Library** group on the **Formulas** tab of the **Ribbon**.

Figure 3.4

Excel guesses which cells you want to sum. Your screen will look like Figure 3.5.

Tip:
It is a good idea to
include cell B10 in
the Sum formula.
If you later need to
add an extra row,
you can insert it
above row 10 and
the Sum formula
will still be correct.

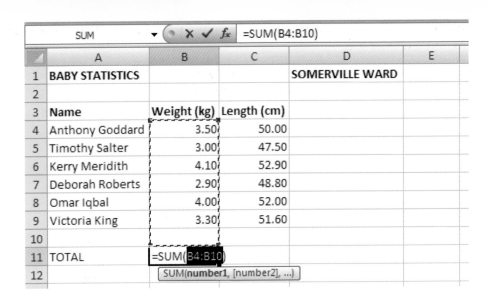

Figure 3.5

▶ Press **Enter**. The answer appears.

▶ Find the total **Length** of all the babies on the ward.

▶ Save your workbook.

In the next chapter we'll look at the other functions such as **Average**, **Minimum** and
Maximum.

Renaming a worksheet

You can change the names of the worksheets to something more meaningful than **Sheet1**
and **Sheet2**.

Figure 3.6

▶ Right click on the **Sheet1** sheet tab.

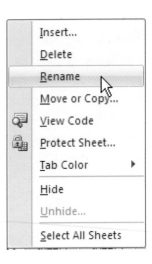

Figure 3.7

◐ Select **Rename** from the shortcut menu that appears. The text on the sheet tab is now selected.

◐ Now type **Birth Stats**. The text will appear on the sheet tab. Just click away from the sheet tab when you have finished typing.

◐ Repeat this for **Sheet2**, renaming it **Daily Weights**.

Inserting and deleting sheets

◐ To delete **Sheet3**, right click the sheet tab then select **Delete** from the shortcut menu that appears.

◐ To insert a new sheet between **Birth Stats** and **Daily Weights**, right click the **Daily Weights** sheet and select **Insert** from the shortcut menu.

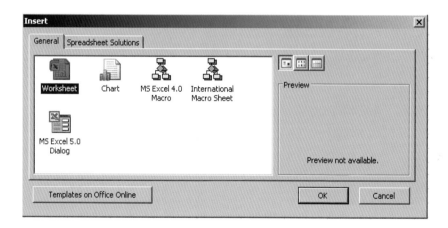

Figure 3.8

◐ Make sure **Worksheet** is selected then click **OK**.

Figure 3.9

Copying a worksheet

You can copy a worksheet within a spreadsheet or between open spreadsheets.

◐ Open a new workbook by clicking the **Office Button** and selecting the **New** icon and then **Blank Workbook**.

◐ You can move from the old workbook (which will be called **Stats** because that was the filename you used when it was saved) and the new workbook (which will probably be called **Book2**) using the **Switch Windows** button on the **View** tab.

Tip:
If you try to delete a worksheet that has data in it, you will see a warning message confirming that you want to delete the sheet.

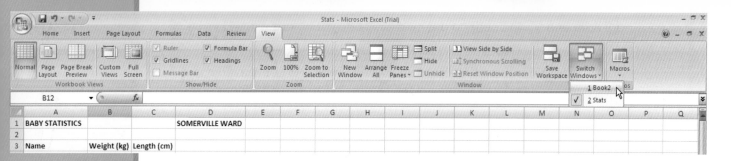

Figure 3.10

In the **Stats** spreadsheet, right click the **Birth Stats** worksheet and select **Move or Copy** from the menu.

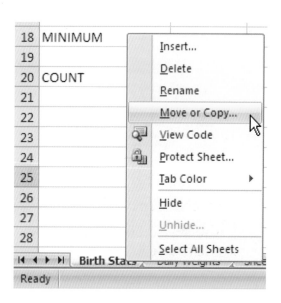

Figure 3.11

You are now asked where you want to copy or move it to.

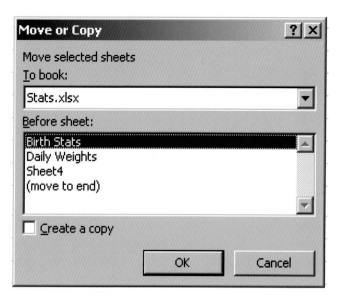

Figure 3.12

▶ In the first drop-down list, select the new workbook you have just opened; it will be called something like **Book2**.

▶ Select where exactly you want the sheet to be put in the second list box. We want to make a copy rather than move it, so click on the **Create a copy** check box.

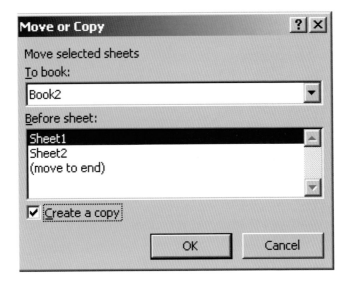

Figure 3.13

Note:
If you wanted to move a worksheet to another workbook you would use the same method, but without clicking the Create a copy check box.

▶ Click **OK**. The worksheet should now be copied to the new workbook.

▶ You can now close the workbook you have just opened (probably called **Book2**). There is no need to save it.

Moving worksheets

▶ You can easily move worksheets by first selecting a sheet, then clicking and dragging it to the new position.

Figure 3.14

Figure 3.15

▶ Save the **Stats** workbook. You will need it again in the next chapter so you don't need to close it.

Chapter 4 – Functions

In this chapter you will continue to work on the **Stats** spreadsheet that you started in the last chapter. You'll learn how to use some of Excel's built-in functions to calculate the **average**, **maximum** and **minimum** baby weights and lengths.

A function is a formula used in a calculation. Excel provides over 200 functions to help with business, scientific and engineering applications. Don't worry, you only need 3 or 4 at this stage!

 Load the spreadsheet **Stats** that you created in the last chapter, if it is not already open.

It should look something like the one below. The **Formula** bar and the **active cell** have been labelled in the screenshot.

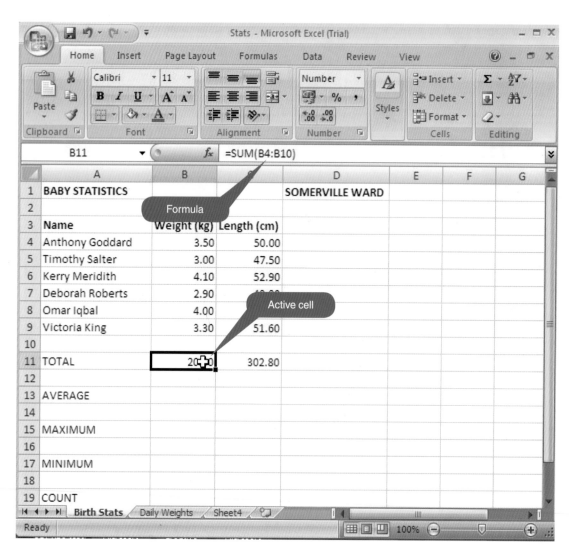

Figure 4.1

The SUM function

You have already used one of Excel's built-in functions – the **SUM** function.

Look at the **Formula** bar in Figure 4.1. It tells you what formula has been used to get the answer **20.80** in the active cell, **B11**.

You entered the **SUM** function by pressing the **AutoSum** button. Adding up a row or column of numbers is such a common task in spreadsheet work that this special shortcut button is provided.

You can also enter a function by typing it into the cell. We'll try that now.

▶ Click in cell **B11**.

▶ Press the **Delete** key to delete the formula currently in the cell.

▶ Repeat this, deleting the formula from cell **C11**.

▶ Type **=sum(** in the **B11** cell (be sure to include the open bracket). You will notice that Excel tries to help by displaying a menu of functions from which you can directly select by double clicking the required function – see Figure 4.2:

	A	B	C	D	E
1	BABY STATISTICS			SOMERVILLE WARD	
2					
3	Name	Weight (kg)	Length (cm)		
4	Anthony Goddard	3.50	50.00		
5	Timothy Salter	3.00	47.50		
6	Kerry Meridith	4.10	52.90		
7	Deborah Roberts	2.90	48.80		
8	Omar Iqbal	4.00	52.00		
9	Victoria King	3.30	51.60		
10					
11	TOTAL	=sum			
12		*fx* SUM	Adds all the numbers in a range of cells		
13	AVERAGE	*fx* SUMIF			
14		*fx* SUMIFS			
15	MAXIMUM	*fx* SUMPRODUCT			
16		*fx* SUMSQ			
17	MINIMUM	*fx* SUMX2MY2			
18		*fx* SUMX2PY2			
19	COUNT	*fx* SUMXMY2			

Figure 4.2

► Now click in cell **B4** and hold the left mouse button down while you drag down to cell **B10**. Notice that Excel is automatically filling in the formula as you do this in both the cell and the **Formula** bar.

► Press the **Enter** button on the keyboard; you don't need to type) to finish the formula.

► Click in cell **B11** again and the formula **=SUM(B4:B10)** appears in the Formula bar as shown in Figure 4.1.

You'll find out why we included the blank cell **B10** in the formula in a minute.

The AVERAGE function

The **AVERAGE** function works in much the same way as the **SUM** function.

► Click in cell **B13**.

► Type **=average(**.

► Again Excel tries to help and you can select the AVERAGE function directly from the displayed menu.

► Click in cell **B4** and drag down to cell **B10**.

► Press **Enter**. The answer, **3.47**, appears in the cell.

► In cell **C13** find the average length of all the babies (it should be **50.47**).

MAX and MIN functions

To find the maximum measurements, you need the **MAX** function.

► Click in cell **B15**.

► Type **=max(** in the cell (including the opening bracket).

► Click in cell **B4** and drag down to cell **B10**.

► Press **Enter**. Note that Excel automatically enters a closing bracket to finish the formula. The answer, **4.10**, appears in the cell.

► Now do the same for the maximum length.

► Use the **MIN** function in the same way to find the minimums.

Your spreadsheet will look like this:

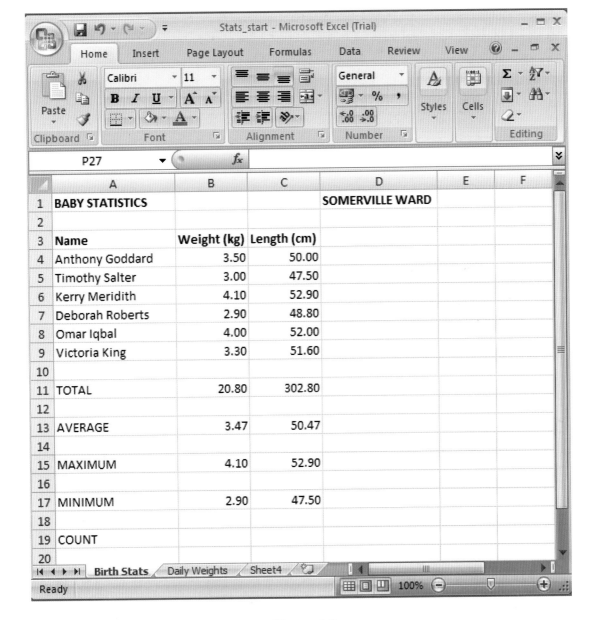

Figure 4.3

The COUNT function

To count the number of babies, you need the COUNT function.

 Click in cell B19.

 Type =count(or select COUNT from the displayed menu, then click in cell B4 then drag down to cell B10 and press Enter.

Excel automatically adds the closing bracket for you. The answer 6.00 should appear in the cell. Notice that although we included 7 rows in the COUNT formula, Excel has only counted those rows where a value has been added.

 Repeat this for the Length column.

 Highlight cells B19 and C19 then click the Decrease Decimal button twice (see Figure 3.4). You can only have whole numbers of babies so we don't need any decimal points!

Adding another record

Suppose another baby is born on the ward and its measurements have to be recorded on the spreadsheet.

 The space you have left in the spreadsheet (**Row 10**) is for this new arrival.

 In **Row 10**, enter the data for **Jacob Walton**, who weighs **3.7kg** and is **51cm** long.

Of course the existing formulas covered **Row 10**, so baby Walton's statistics are included in the updating of **TOTAL**, **AVERAGE**, **MAXIMUM**, **MINIMUM** and **COUNT**. But there has been another happy event! Welcome into the world **Alison Hemmingway**, weighing in at **3.9kg** and **51.7cm** long. There no space left for her data to be added, so we need to insert a row:

 Right click the row header for row **11**. The shortcut menu will appear (see Figure 4.4).

	A	B	C	D
1	**BABY STATISTICS**			**SOMERVILLE WARD**
2				
3	**Name**	**Weight (kg)**	**Length (cm)**	
4	Anthony Goddard	3.50	50.00	
5	Timothy Salter	3.00	47.50	
6	Kerry Meridith	4.10	52.90	
7	Deborah Roberts	2.90	48.80	
8	Omar Iqbal	4.00	52.00	
9	Victoria King	3.30	51.60	
10	Jacob Watson	3.70	51.00	
11	TOTAL	24.50	353.80	
12	✂ Cut			
13	📋 Copy		50.54	
14	📋 Paste			
15	Paste Special...		52.90	
16	Insert			
17	Delete		47.50	
18	Clear Contents			
19	Format Cells...		7.0	
20				
21	Row Height...			
22	Hide			
23	Unhide			
24				

Figure 4.4

Select **Insert** from the menu to insert a new row.

In the new row, enter the data for **Alison Hemmingway**. After entering each statistic, press **Enter**. You will see Excel update each of the formulas in turn.

Click in cell **B12** and look at the formula in the formula bar. The formula has automatically adjusted to include the new row and its new data – which saves us having to change it! Further checks on the other formulas will reveal that they too have been updated. Remember that it was the addition of data to the row which triggered the update, not the insertion of the new row.

Now we'll double-underline the title **Baby Statistics**.

Select cell **A1** then click in the selection with the right mouse button.

Select **Format Cells** from the shortcut menu.

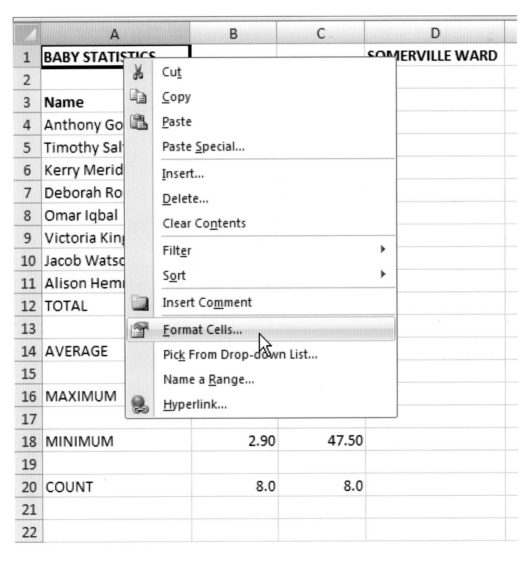

Figure 4.5

Click the **Font** tab. Now choose **Double** from the list in the **Underline** box.

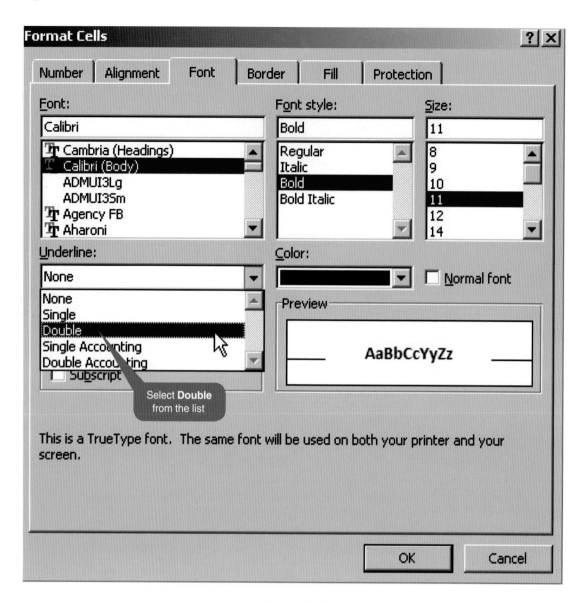

Figure 4.6

Click **OK**. The spreadsheet will now look like this:

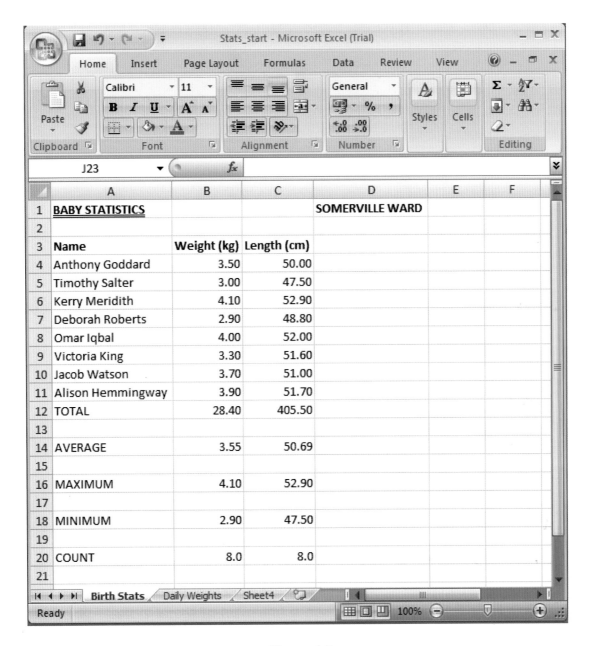

Figure 4.7

If your spreadsheet looks different from this, check the formulas.

 Save your spreadsheet.

Copying data between sheets

On another sheet in the workbook we are going to create a chart to record the weights of all the babies over the first 5 days. We can copy the titles and names of all the babies to save us typing them in again.

 Make sure the **Birth Stats** sheet is selected. Select cells **A1** to **D1**.

 Click the **Copy** button on the **Home** tab of the **Ribbon**.

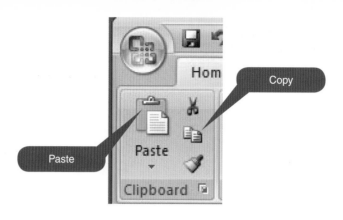

Figure 4.8

▶ Click the **Daily Weights** sheet tab to go to the second sheet.

▶ Click in cell **A1** to make it the active cell.

▶ Click the **Paste** button.

▶ Copy cells **A3** to **A11** from **Birth Stats** to **Daily Weights**. You'll need to widen column **A** to fit the names and title.

▶ In cell **B3** type **Day 1**.

▶ Click in row header **3** to select the row. Use the **Bold** button to make all the cells bold. (You may have to press it twice.)

Now your worksheet should look similar to Figure 4.9.

	A	B	C	D	E	F	G
1	**BABY STATISTICS**			**SOMMERVILLE WARD**			
2							
3	**Name**	**Day 1**					
4	Anthony Goddard						
5	Timothy Salter						
6	Kerry Meridith						
7	Deborah Roberts						
8	Omar Iqbal						
9	Victoria King						
10	Jacob Walton						
11	Alison Hemmingway						
12							

Birth Stats | **Daily Weights** | Sheet4

Figure 4.9

Filling a series

Instead of typing all the other days, Day 2, Day 3 etc. in cells **C3** to **F3**, you can let Excel do it for you.

▶ Click cell **B3**.

▶ Click and drag the small black handle in the bottom right-hand corner of the cell. This is called the **Fill handle**. Drag it to cell **F3**.

Figure 4.10

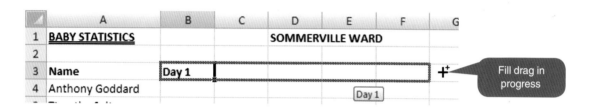

Figure 4.11

Now your headings should look like this:

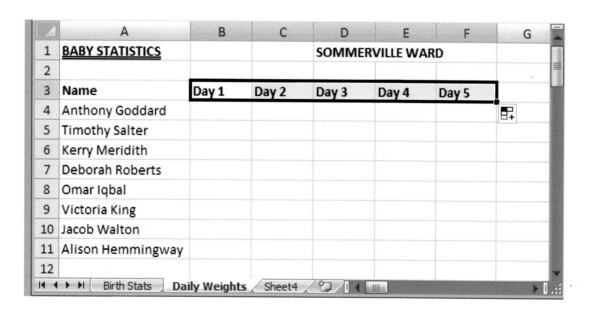

Figure 4.12

▶ Save your workbook.

Hide or unhide rows and columns

Hiding rows and columns is useful if you don't want certain data to appear on a print-out, or simply to make data in a large spreadsheet easier to view on screen.

Hiding rows

We'll hide the **TOTAL** row (row **12**) in the **Stats** spreadsheet.

▶ Click on the **Birth Stats** tab to make it the active sheet.

▶ Click the row header for row **12**. This highlights the whole row.

▶ Right click in the highlighted row to reveal the shortcut menu as shown in Figure 4.13.

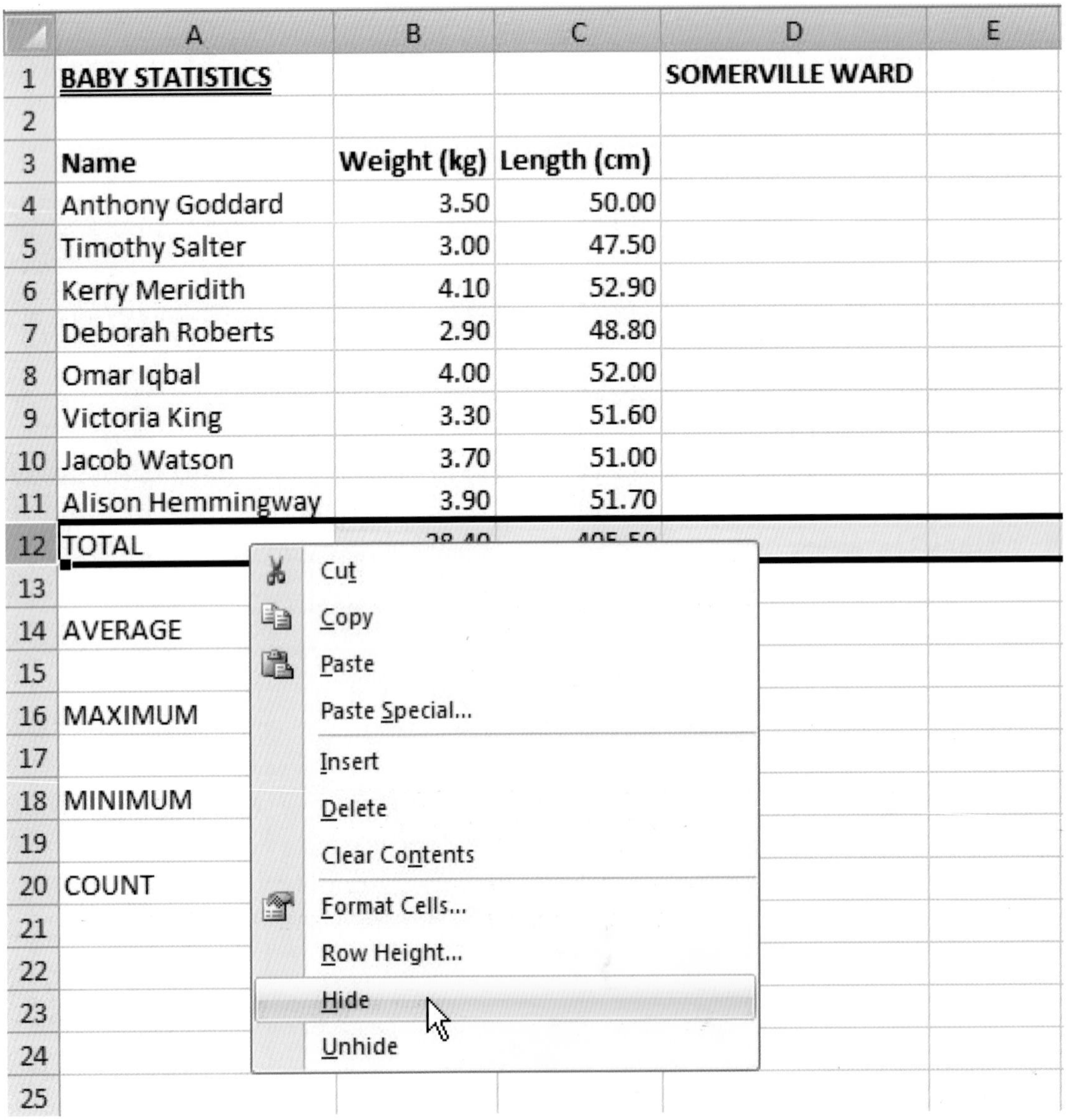

	A	B	C	D	E
1	**BABY STATISTICS**			**SOMERVILLE WARD**	
2					
3	**Name**	**Weight (kg)**	**Length (cm)**		
4	Anthony Goddard	3.50	50.00		
5	Timothy Salter	3.00	47.50		
6	Kerry Meridith	4.10	52.90		
7	Deborah Roberts	2.90	48.80		
8	Omar Iqbal	4.00	52.00		
9	Victoria King	3.30	51.60		
10	Jacob Watson	3.70	51.00		
11	Alison Hemmingway	3.90	51.70		
12	TOTAL	28.40	405.50		
13					
14	AVERAGE				
15					
16	MAXIMUM				
17					
18	MINIMUM				
19					
20	COUNT				
21					
22					
23					
24					
25					

Shortcut menu:
- ✂ Cut
- 📋 Copy
- 📋 Paste
- Paste Special...
- Insert
- Delete
- Clear Contents
- 🖉 Format Cells...
- Row Height...
- Hide
- Unhide

Figure 4.13

▶ Select **Hide**.

Row 12 is now hidden – notice that there is no row **12** row header.

Unhiding rows

 Select the row headers for rows **11** and **13** by clicking on one and dragging across the other (see Figure 4.14). Both rows are now highlighted.

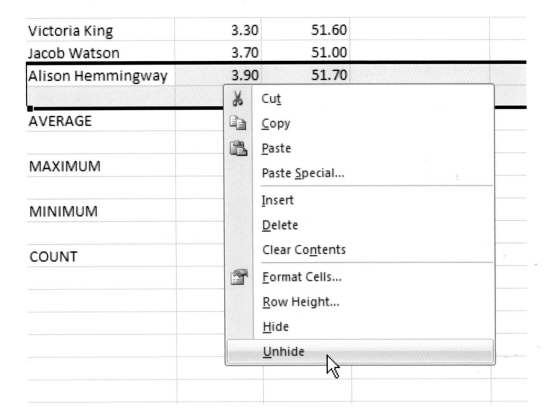

Victoria King	3.30	51.60
Jacob Watson	3.70	51.00
Alison Hemmingway	3.90	51.70
AVERAGE		
MAXIMUM		
MINIMUM		
COUNT		

Menu:
- ✂ Cut
- 📋 Copy
- 📋 Paste
- Paste Special...
- Insert
- Delete
- Clear Contents
- 🗔 Format Cells...
- Row Height...
- Hide
- Unhide

Figure 4.14

 Right click anywhere in the highlighted rows and select **Unhide** from the menu.

Row 12 should now be visible.

Hiding and unhiding columns

These processes are exactly the same as for rows:

 Hide column **C** by clicking in its column header, then right click anywhere in the highlighted column and select **Hide** from the menu.

 Unhide column **C** by selecting the column headers for both columns **B** and **D**, then right click anywhere in the highlighted columns and select **Unhide** from the menu.

Freeze row and column titles

In a big spreadsheet, it is useful to have the row and column titles frozen so that no matter where you scroll in the spreadsheet you can see them.

First we'll make the **Stats** spreadsheet a bit bigger.

- Make **Daily Weights** the active sheet.

- Starting in cell **F3**, use the **Fill Handle** to extend the headings to **Day 50**.

- Click in cell **A12** and type **Baby 1**. Use the fill handle to enter babies **2** to **50**.

- To freeze the row and column titles, you have to place the cursor in **the nearest cell to A1 that you don't want frozen**. That sounds like a bit of a mouthful! Basically, we need column **A** frozen, and row **3** frozen. For this we need to make cell **B4** the active cell.

- Select the **View** tab on the **Ribbon** and then click the **Freeze Panes** button in the **Window** group. Select the **Freeze Panes** option from the menu.

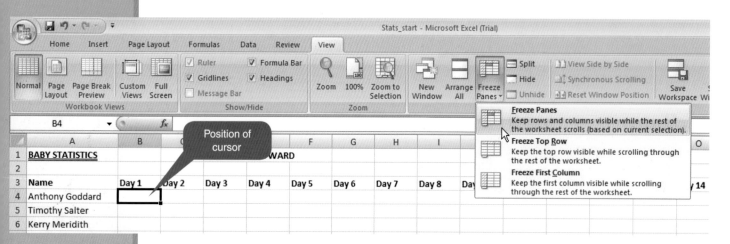

Figure 4.15

Black lines will appear next to the frozen panes.

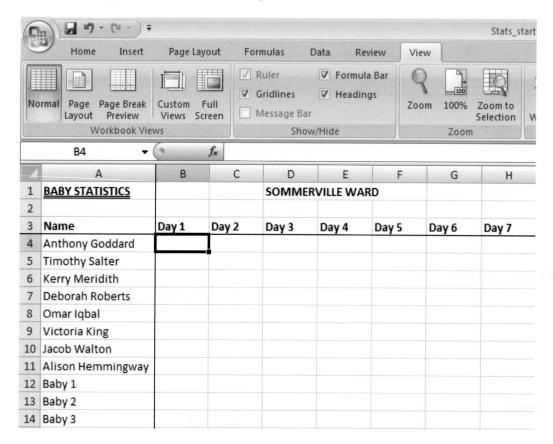

Figure 4.16

▶ Scroll across to **Day 50** – the baby names should still be visible. This would be invaluable for anyone entering data as otherwise they would have to scroll left to see which baby was in each row before entering the data.

▶ Now try scrolling down to **Baby 50** to see the effect of the frozen column headings.

Unfreezing panes

▶ Click the **Freeze Panes** button and select **Unfreeze Panes** from the menu. It doesn't matter which cell is the active cell for this. The black lines will disappear.

Opening several workbooks

This is very straightforward. You can open a second spreadsheet in just the same way you did the first.

With the **Stats** spreadsheet open, either

▶ Click on the **Office Button** and select **New**, *or*

▶ Hold down the **Ctrl** key on the keyboard and press the **N** key.

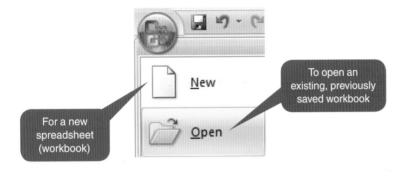

Figure 4.17

▶ To flick between workbooks, swap to the **View** tab on the **Ribbon** and click the **Switch Windows** button. You can now select the worksheet that you wish to see and work with from the drop-down list, or

▶ Use the buttons at the bottom of your screen.

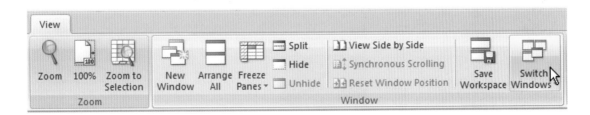

Figure 4.18

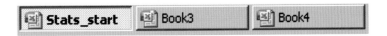

Figure 4.19

41

Saving under another name

▶ To save an existing workbook under a different name, open the workbook then select the **Office Button**, **Save As** from the menu and then **Excel Workbook** (see Figure 4.20).

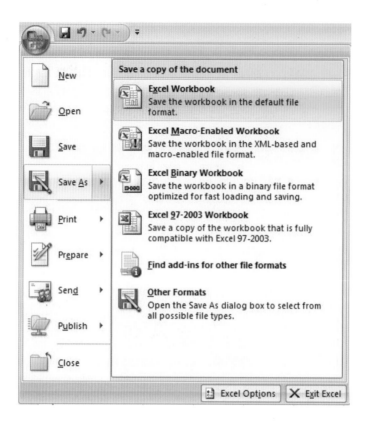

Figure 4.20

▶ You will then be asked where you want to save it and what name you want to save it under (see Figure 4.21).

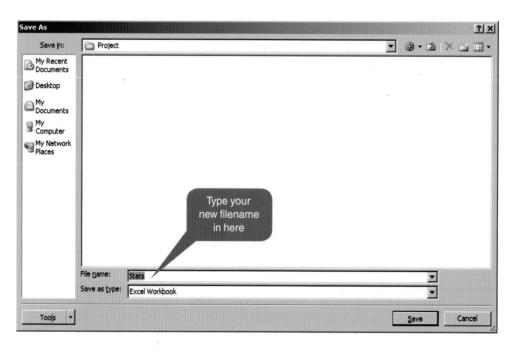

Figure 4.21

Saving as a different file type

By default, Excel will save your workbooks as **.xlsx** files, but you can choose from many other file types, for instance you want to alter the file type saved to enable it to be used on a computer which has different spreadsheet software or an earlier version of Excel.

▶ To save a file as a different file type, select **File**, **Save As** from the menu.

▶ Type a name for the file in the **File name** box, and choose a folder location for the file.

▶ Click the down-arrow in the **Save as type** box to view all the different file types. Select the one you want, then click **Save**.

▶ Close the **Stats** workbook.

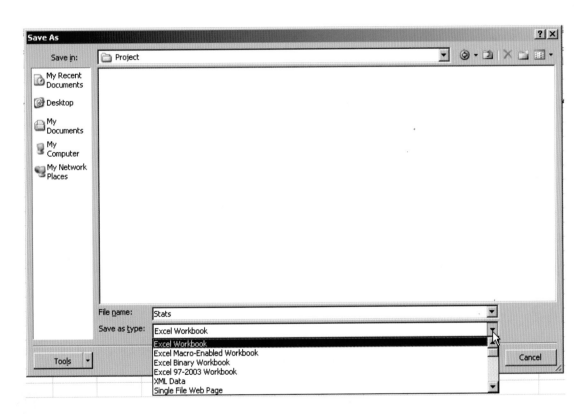

Figure 4.22

Chapter 5 – Charts

Charts are a very good way of presenting information so that it is easy to grasp immediately.

In this chapter we'll look at how the number of songbirds in the UK has declined over the past 3 decades.

This alarming decline is partly due to modern farming methods. Many hedgerows, meadows and marshes have disappeared, so birds have nowhere to live. Chemicals sprayed on fields kill insects that birds need for food.

Project: Draw charts relating to the number of songbirds in England

Decline in songbird numbers between 1972 and 1996 (Numbers given in millions)	1972	1996
Skylark	7.72	3.09
Willow warbler	6.06	4.67
Linnet	1.56	0.925
Song thrush	3.62	1.74
Lapwing	0.588	0.341
Yellowhammer	4.4	1.76
Blackbird	12.54	8.4
Tree sparrow	0.65	0.0845
Corn bunting	0.144	0.03
Source: British Trust for Ornithology		

Table 5.1

Open a new workbook.

Type the headings and the names of the birds in the survey as shown in Figure 5.1.

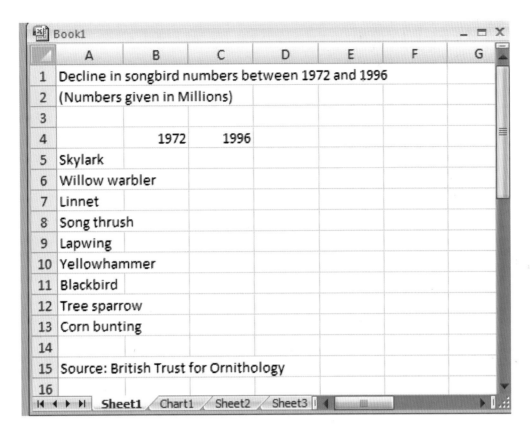

	A	B	C	D	E	F	G
1	Decline in songbird numbers between 1972 and 1996						
2	(Numbers given in Millions)						
3							
4		1972	1996				
5	Skylark						
6	Willow warbler						
7	Linnet						
8	Song thrush						
9	Lapwing						
10	Yellowhammer						
11	Blackbird						
12	Tree sparrow						
13	Corn bunting						
14							
15	Source: British Trust for Ornithology						
16							

Sheet1   Chart1   Sheet2   Sheet3

Figure 5.1

Position the mouse pointer between the column headers for **A** and **B**. Drag to the right to widen column **A**.

Click in row header **1**, and hold down the **Ctrl** key while you click in row headers **4** and **15**. This selects all three rows.

Click the **Bold** button in the **Font** group of the **Home** tab on the **Ribbon** to make the text in these rows bold.

Click in cell **A15** and press the **Italic** button to make it italic.

Enter the rest of the data given in Table 5.1.

When you have done that, your spreadsheet will look like this:

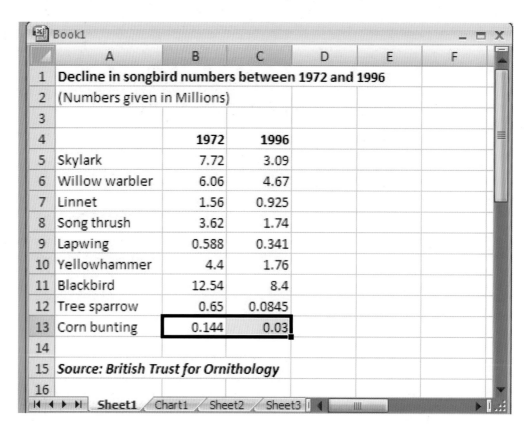

Figure 5.2

▶ Save your workbook, naming it **Birds**.

Sorting data

It would be neater if the birds were sorted in alphabetical order.

▶ First we need to select the data we want to sort. Click to select cell **A5** and drag to cell **C13**.

▶ Launch the **Sort** dialogue box by selecting the **Data** tab on the **Ribbon**, and then the **Sort** button in the **Sort and Filter** group (see Figure 5.3).

▶ We want to sort by the bird names, which are in column **A**. Fill in the boxes as shown below.

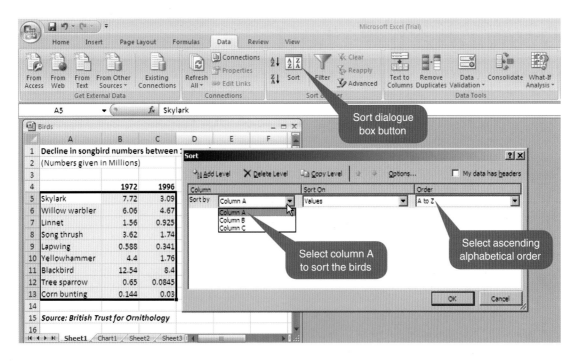

Figure 5.3

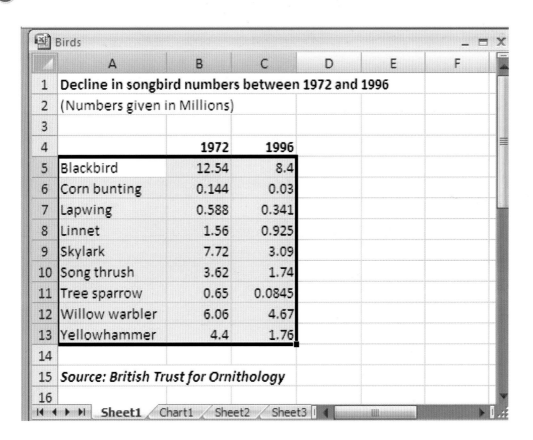

> Click **OK**. The names should now be sorted.

Figure 5.4

Drawing a bar chart

Now we can draw a bar chart to show this data. Note that we are actually producing a graph, but Excel prefers to use the word 'chart'.

▶ Click in cell **A4** and drag diagonally through to **C13** to select the cells to be charted.

▶ Select the **Insert** tab on the **Ribbon** and click the **Column** button in the **Charts** group.

You will see a dialogue box like the one in Figure 5.5.

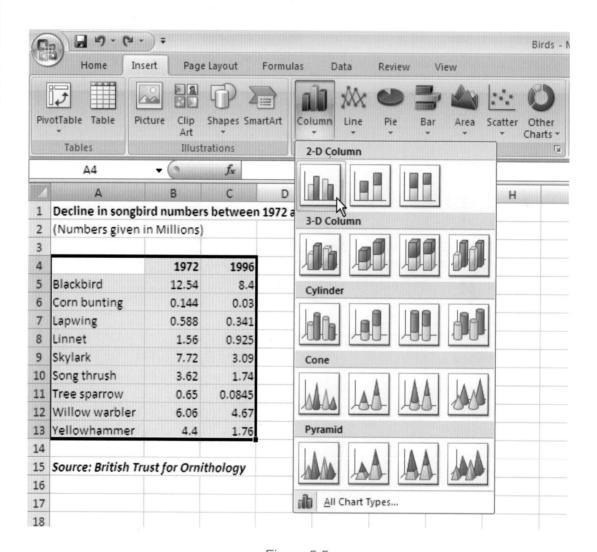

Figure 5.5

▶ In the dialogue box select **2-D Column** and click the **Clustered Column** option; the chart will open (Figure 5.6):

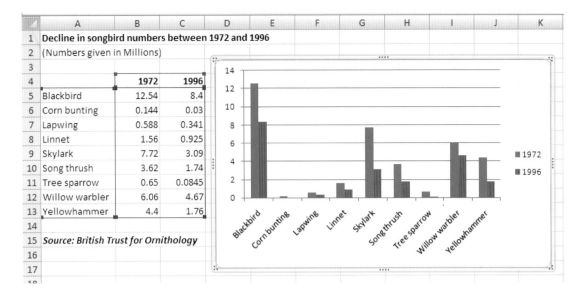

Figure 5.6

Adding a title

▶ Swap to the **Chart Tools Layout** tab, click the **Chart title** button and select the position for the chart title:

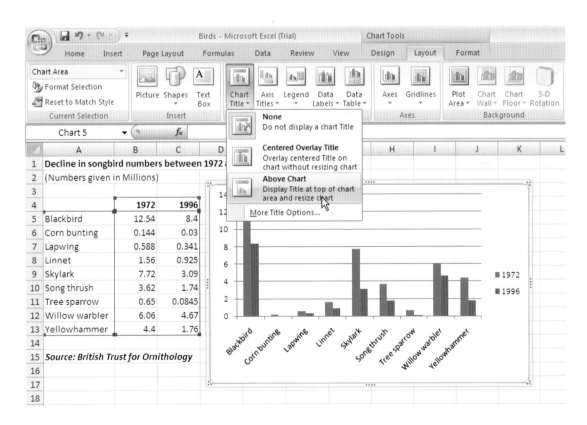

Figure 5.7

▶ Type the title in the **Formula** bar and press **Enter**. The text appears in the Chart Title, see Figure 5.8. If you wish to alter the font size or type, highlight the title, move to the Home tab and alter the font in the usual way.

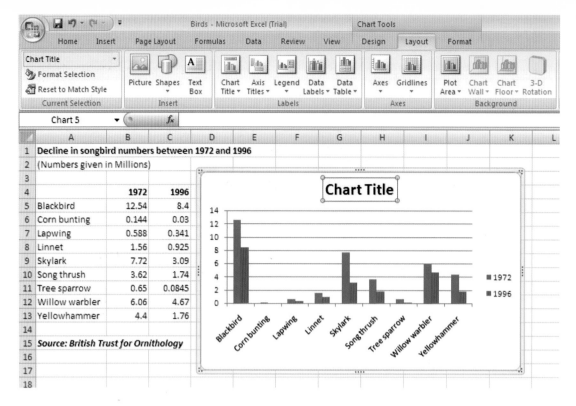

Figure 5.8

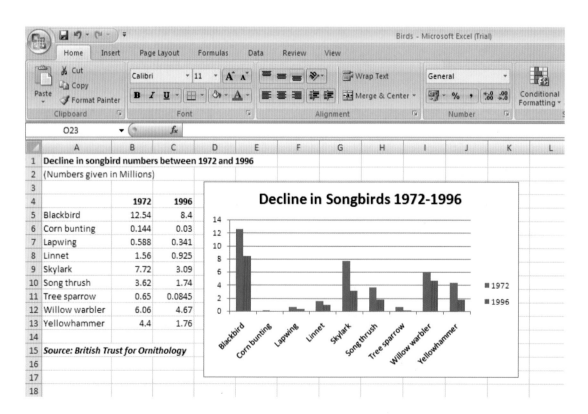

The chart will look something like that in Figure 5.9:

Figure 5.9

Deleting the title

▶ This is very straightforward. Just click the chart title and press the **Delete** key.

▶ To reinstate the title, use the **Undo** button on the **Quick Access Toolbar**.

Moving and sizing a chart

You can move the chart so that it does not overlap the data and is positioned suitably for printing, for instance, so it can fit on a single page for printing.

▶ Move the mouse pointer to just inside the line round the chart. This is the chart area and you should find that the mouse pointer turns into a cross shape of pointers. Click and drag the chart to the new location.

▶ Move the mouse pointer over the chart, letting the pointer rest for a few seconds on each object. Notice that the **tool tip** tells you what each part of the chart is called.

▶ See if you can identify the parts of the chart called **chart area**, **plot area**, **category axis**, **value axis**, **series '1972'** and **series '1996'**.

▶ Click in the **chart area** and drag the chart below the data.

▶ Drag the bottom right-hand corner handle of the chart to make it bigger. To make it bigger without distorting the shape of the graph, press the **Shift** key while dragging the handle.

▶ Right click on one of the axes. Edit the font size using the **Font** option from the shortcut menu and then select **Size**. If you increase the size of the font, make sure all the category names appear on the axis.

Tip:
If you right click the chart title, legend or either axis, a shortcut menu will appear. The font used can be changed using the Font option and other features changed using the Format option.

Adding axis titles

It would be nice to have an axis title on the **Y** axis, to make it clear that the figures are in millions. The process of adding this is similar to that of adding a title to the chart.

▶ Select **Chart Tools**, **Layout** on the **Ribbon** and then click the **Axis Titles** button (see Figure 5.10).

Figure 5.10

▶ Select **Primary Vertical Axis Title** and then **Rotated Title** from the options (see Figure 5.11).

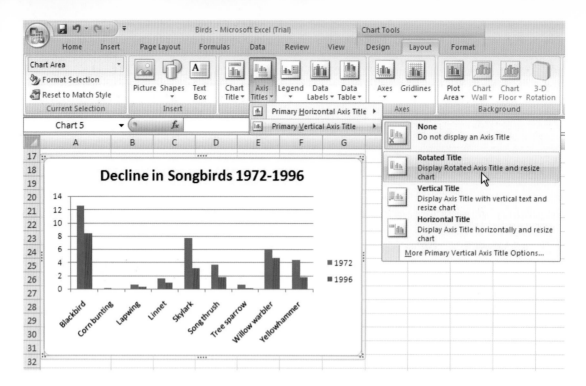

Figure 5.11

Type **Millions** in the **Formula** bar and press the **Enter** key.

The axis title 'Millions' appears, arranged vertically, on the chart next to the vertical axis.

Changing the background colour

Place the cursor over the **Plot Area**. If you're not sure which part of the chart is the **Plot Area**, just leave the mouse pointer over part of it for a few seconds and the **tool tip** should tell you what the pointer is over. If this doesn't happen, it is likely that the chart is not active and you will need to select it by clicking its outline.

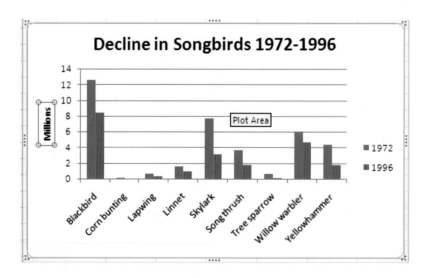

Figure 5.12

Right click with the mouse. A shortcut menu appears.

➤ Select **Format Plot Area** from the menu.

Here you can change both the border style and colour, and the background colour.

➤ Have a play with the settings, and try giving the chart a different background colour. Click **OK**.

Changing the colour of the bars

You have to change the colour of the 1972 series separately from the 1996 series. We'll start by changing the 1972 series.

➤ Place the mouse over any bar in the 1972 series. After a few seconds the tool tip should say **Series '1972'** followed by the bird name and the value of the particular bar you are on.

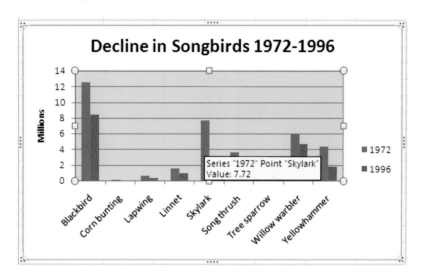

Figure 5.13

➤ Right click with the mouse. The shortcut menu appears.

➤ Select **Format Data Series** from the menu.

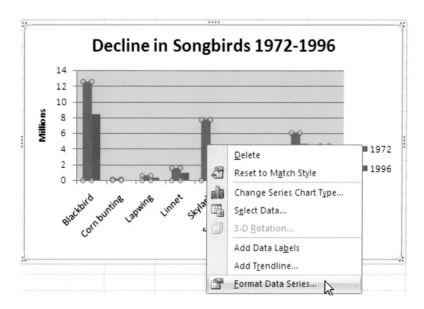

Figure 5.14

The **Format Data Series** window appears (see Figure 5.15). Here you can change the border around each bar and the fill colour of the bars.

▶ Select **Fill** and then choose **Solid fill**. You can now choose a new fill colour by clicking a colour from the **colour palette** displayed. Click **Close**.

▶ Now repeat this for the 1996 series. Follow exactly the same method, but just make sure that you right click on the 1996 series to start.

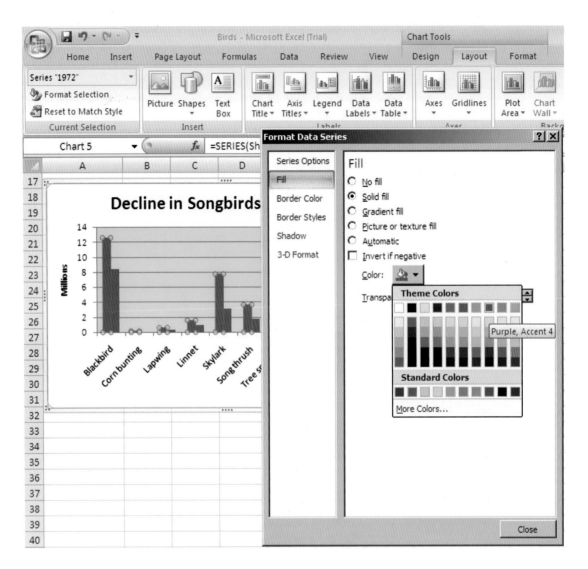

Figure 5.15

▶ There are many opportunities for experimentation, such as graduated fills, and you could spend some time trying these out.

▶ When you are happy with the way the chart looks, save your spreadsheet.

Chapter 6 – Pie Charts

Creating a pie chart

We'll use another sheet in the same workbook to enter some data from the RSPB 2003 Garden Bird Watch Survey. We will then use this data to create a **pie chart**.

▶ Make sure the **Birds** workbook is open.

▶ Click on the tab for **Sheet2**.

▶ Enter the following data.

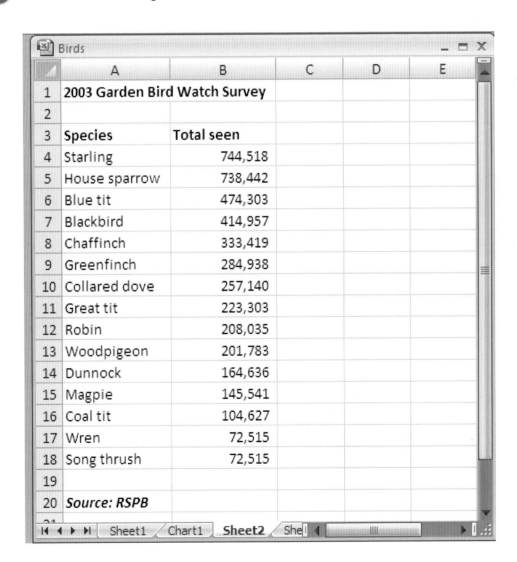

	A	B	C	D	E
1	2003 Garden Bird Watch Survey				
2					
3	Species	Total seen			
4	Starling	744,518			
5	House sparrow	738,442			
6	Blue tit	474,303			
7	Blackbird	414,957			
8	Chaffinch	333,419			
9	Greenfinch	284,938			
10	Collared dove	257,140			
11	Great tit	223,303			
12	Robin	208,035			
13	Woodpigeon	201,783			
14	Dunnock	164,636			
15	Magpie	145,541			
16	Coal tit	104,627			
17	Wren	72,515			
18	Song thrush	72,515			
19					
20	Source: RSPB				

Sheet1 / Chart1 / **Sheet2** / She

Figure 6.1

Drag across cells **A4** to **B18** to select them.

Swap to the **Insert** tab on the **Ribbon** and click the **Pie** button in the **Chart** group.

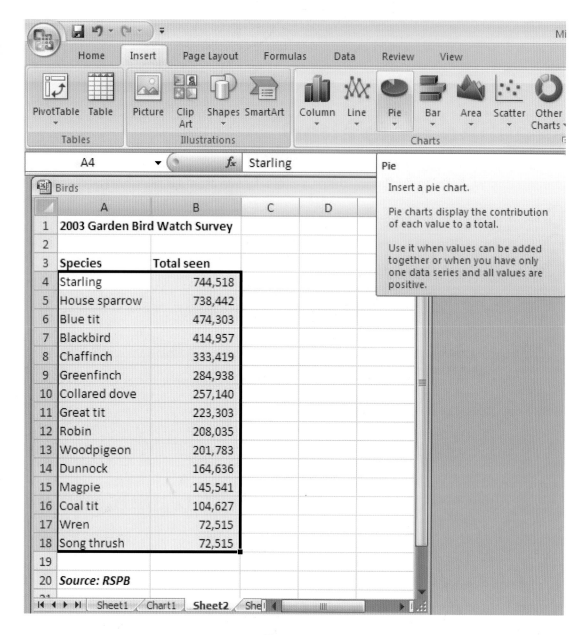

Figure 6.2

Select the basic pie chart from those offered – see Figure 6.3.

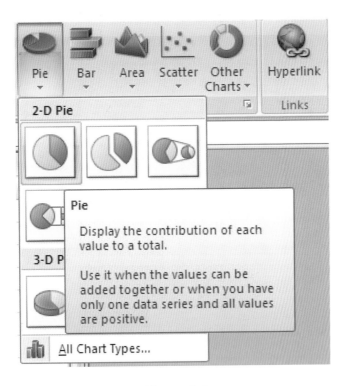

Figure 6.3

 The basic pie chart opens in the spreadsheet.

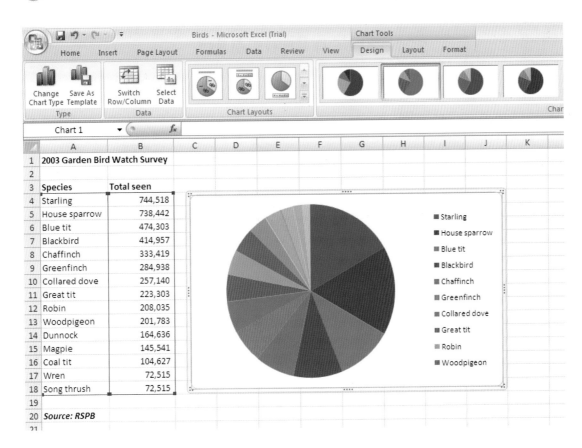

Figure 6.4

▶ Swap to the **Chart Tools Layout** tab on the **Ribbon** and click the **Chart Title** button. Select the **Above Chart** option for the position of the title in the chart.

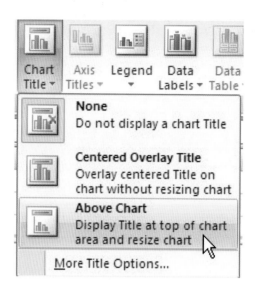

Figure 6.5

▶ Type the title in the **Formula** bar and press enter. You can, as an alternative, click in the **Chart Title** text box and delete the placeholder text **Chart Title** and type in the new title. Highlight the title and use the font editing facilities on the **Home** tab to alter the font type, size etc.

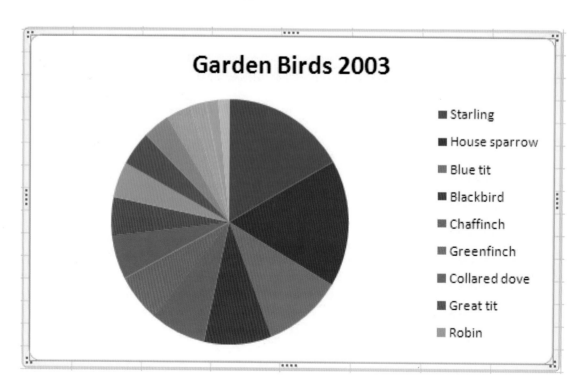

Figure 6.6

Let's add some labels to identify the slices of the pie chart. At the moment **Data Labels** is set to **None** so we need to turn on this facility.

▶ Swap to the **Chart Tools Layout** tab on the **Ribbon** and click the **Data Labels** button, select the **More Data Labels Options** from the drop-down menu.

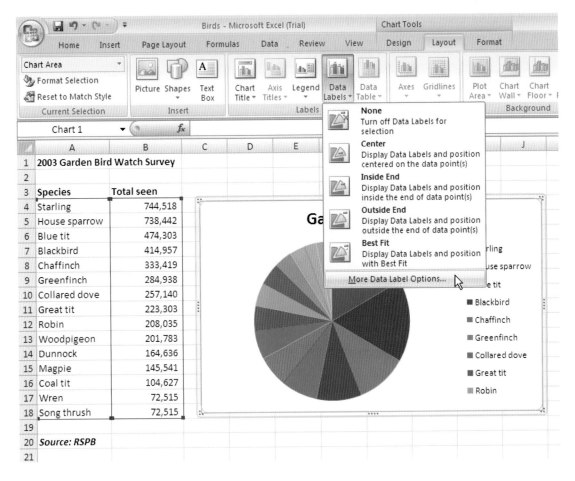

Figure 6.7

The **Format Data Labels** dialogue box opens. Move it to the right by clicking on its **title bar** and dragging with the mouse, so that you can see the result of your changes to selections in the **Format Data Labels** dialogue box.

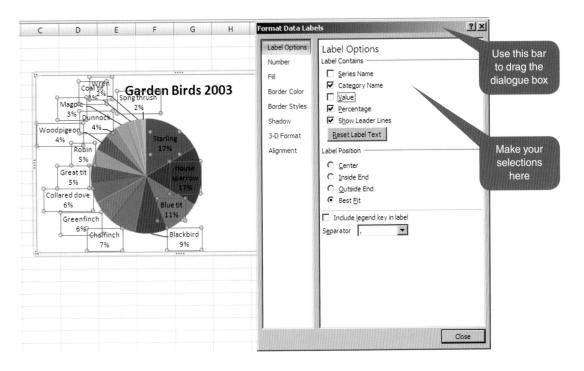

Figure 6.8

Note:
Don't worry if the labels are muddled – we'll fix this later.

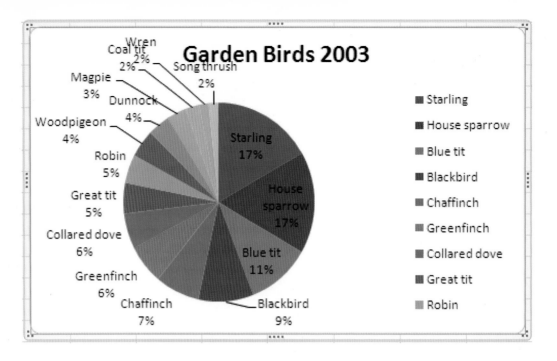

Figure 6.9

▶ Swap to the **Chart Tools Design** tab and click the **Move Chart** button in the **Location** group.

▶ This time we will place the chart in a separate **Chart sheet**. Click **New sheet** in the **Move Chart** dialogue box.

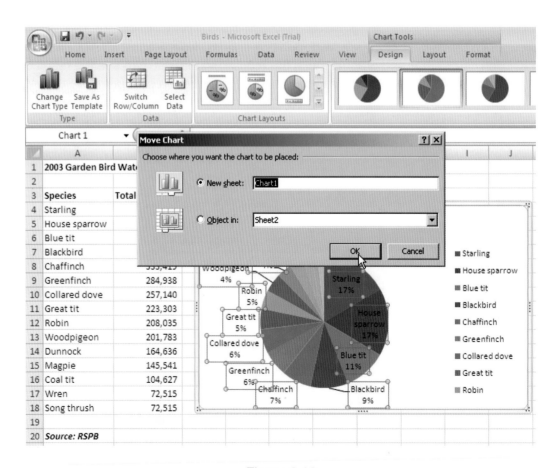

Figure 6.10

Click **OK**.

The chart appears in a new chart sheet.

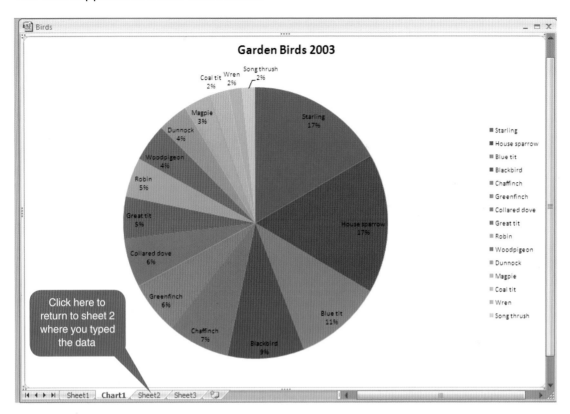

Figure 6.11

Formatting the data labels

We need to make the labels a bit bigger – they're too small to read!

 Right click on any of the data labels.

 A shortcut menu appears. Click **Font** (Figure 6.12).

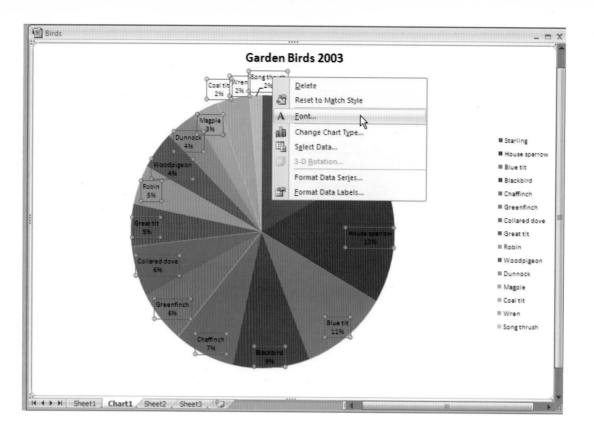

Figure 6.12

▷ This brings up the **Font** dialogue box.

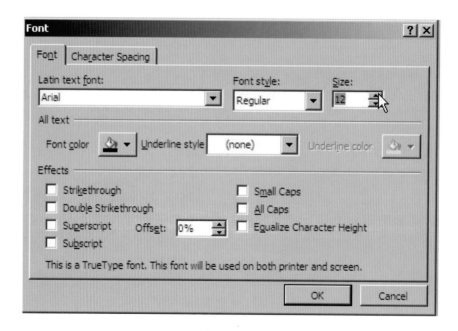

Figure 6.13

▷ Change the font to **Arial** and the size to **12** point. Click **OK**.

▷ If any labels are overlapping, click on them and drag them away from each other.

▷ Format the legend so the text is **12** point.

▷ Format the **Chart Title** to **18** point and move it so that it does not interfere with the data labels.

▶ Change the title to **Garden Bird Numbers 2003**.

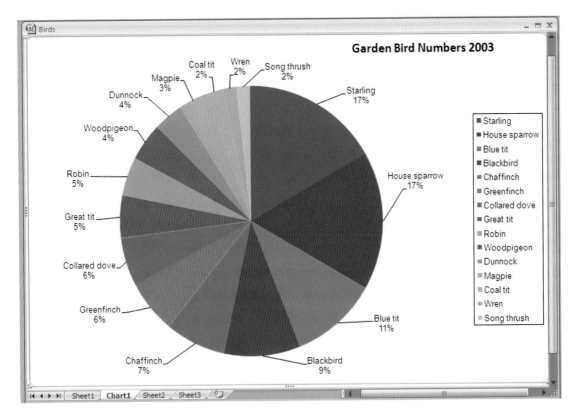

Figure 6.14

▶ Save your workbook.

Copying and pasting charts

We'll copy and paste the pie chart onto a new sheet.

▶ Click once on the **Chart Area** of the pie chart (this is the white background – as Figure 6.15 shows, if you leave the cursor over it for a few seconds, the tool tip will come up) to select it.

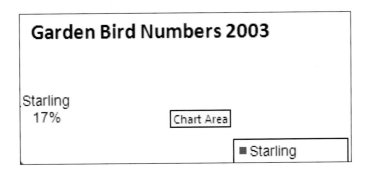

Figure 6.15

▶ Select the **Copy** button on the **Home** tab (Figure 6.16).

Figure 6.16

▶ Click on **Sheet3** at the bottom of the screen to select it and make it the active sheet. Now select the **Paste** button on the **Home** tab (see Figure 6.16).

The pie chart is pasted into **Sheet3**. It's much bigger than we want it so now we'll resize it.

▶ Scroll down so that you can see the bottom right-hand corner of the chart. There should be a small black handle in the corner. If there isn't, try clicking the chart to select it.

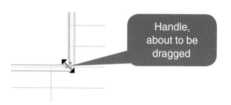

Figure 6.17

▶ Click and drag the handle towards the top left corner while holding down the **Shift** key, until the chart is a similar size to the one shown in Figure 6.18.

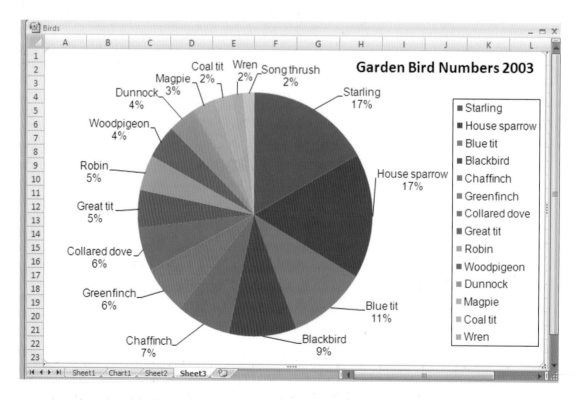

Figure 6.18

64

Changing the chart type

It's easy to change the chart type, for example from a pie chart to a bar or line chart, even after you have created it.

▶ Make sure **Sheet3** is selected. Change to the **Chart Tools Design** tab and click the **Change Chart Type** button.

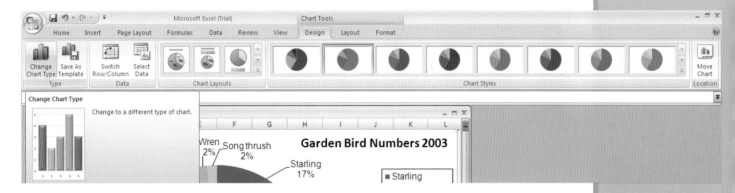

Figure 6.19

▶ The **Change Chart Type** dialogue box appears (see Figure 6.20).

▶ Here all you need to do is choose another chart type. Try a **Line** chart. Click **OK**.

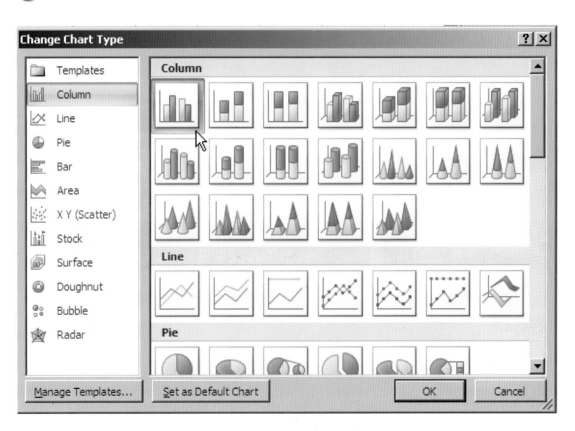

Figure 6.20

It doesn't actually make any sense to make this chart a line chart. Line charts should only be used when the order of the categories along the x-axis has a meaning and where intervening values can exist, such as changes of temperature at different time intervals. In this example, midway points, for example, between **Starling** and **House sparrow**, have no meaning. You can't have a number of birds of a species midway between a **Starling** and **House sparrow**.

▶ Change the chart type to a column chart.

▶ Delete the labels above each column by right clicking on a column and selecting **Format Data Labels** from the shortcut menu. Refer to the section above which guided you through inserting the labels into the pie chart if you need to.

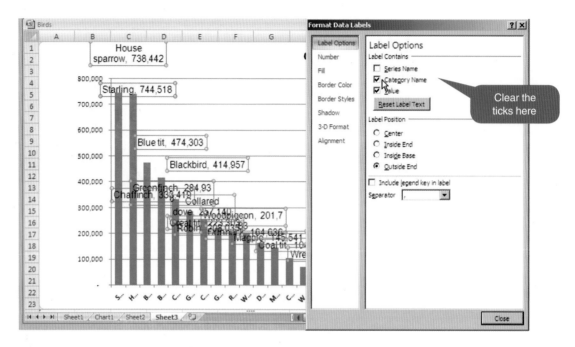

Figure 6.21

Deleting a chart

▶ Now delete the bar chart on **Sheet3** by clicking it to select it, then pressing the **Delete** key.

▶ Save your workbook.

Chapter 7 – Printing

Now we're going to try printing various parts from the **Birds** workbook.

 Make sure the **Birds** workbook is open.

 Click **Sheet1** to select it.

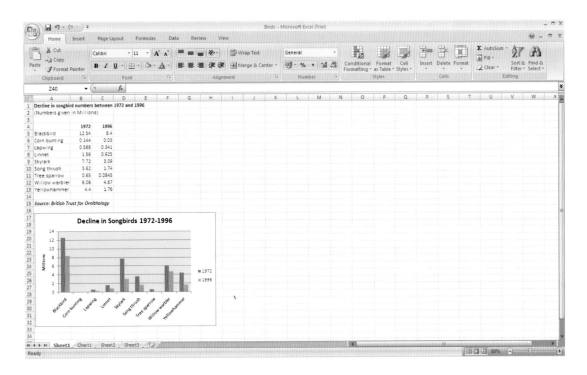

Figure 7.1

Printing a chart

Firstly we'll see what the chart would look like printed on its own.

 Make sure the chart is selected. (It will have handles around it if it is – see Figure 7.2. Click the **Chart Area** to select it if it is not already selected.)

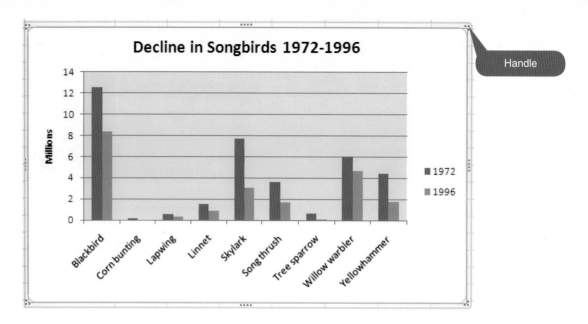

Handle

Figure 7.2

▶ Click the **Office** button, select **Print** and then **Print Preview**. This shows you how your chart will look when it is printed.

Figure 7.3

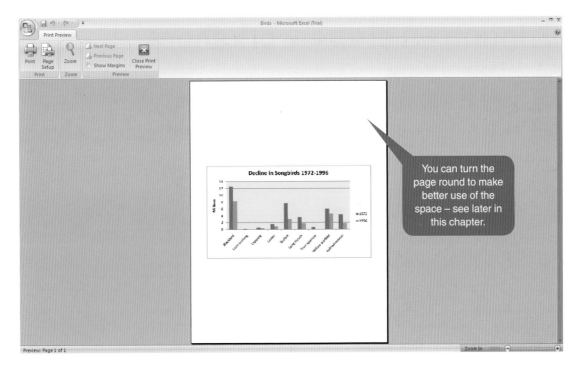

Figure 7.4

▶ Now click the **Print** button at the top left of the screen. This closes the **Print Preview** window and opens the **Print** dialogue box.

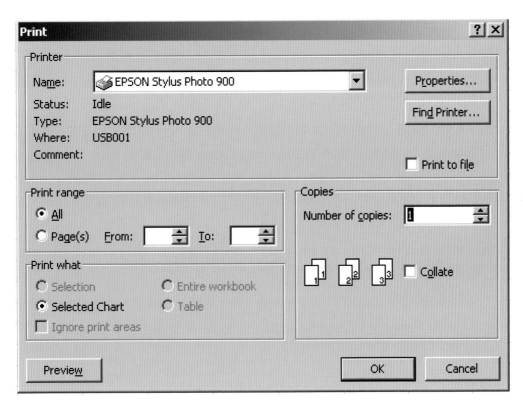

Figure 7.5

▶ You can change various options here such as the number of copies and which printer to print on.

▶ When you are happy with the options, click **OK** to print.

Printing an entire worksheet

▷ Click away from the chart to deselect it.

▷ Click the **Office** button and then select **Print** and then **Print Preview**.

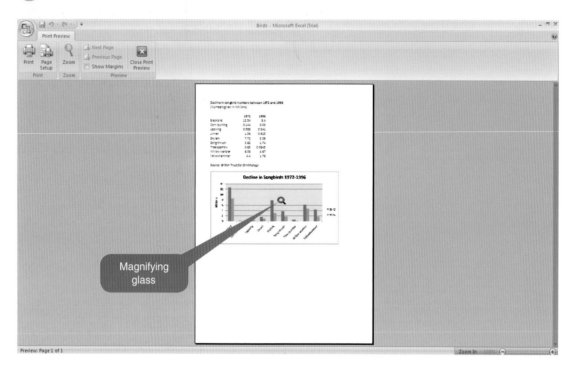

Figure 7.6

▷ When you move the pointer over the page, it changes to a magnifying glass. Click it to zoom in on the page.

▷ Click **Print** at the top left of the screen to launch the **Print** dialogue box.

▷ When you are happy with the various options, click **OK** to print.

Printing a cell range

You can specify the cell range that you want to print. We'll use this method to print only the figures on **Sheet1**, without the chart.

▷ Click cell **A1** and drag across to cell **F15** – these are the cells we want to print.

▷ Swap to the **Page Layout** tab, click the **Print Area** button and select **Set Print Area** from the shortcut menu.

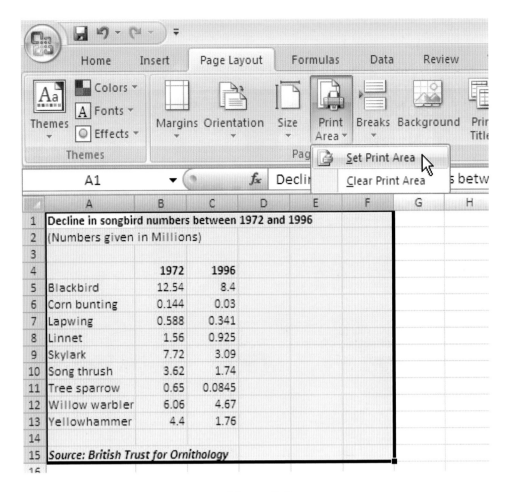

Figure 7.7

▶ Click the **Office button** and then select **Print** and then **Print Preview**.

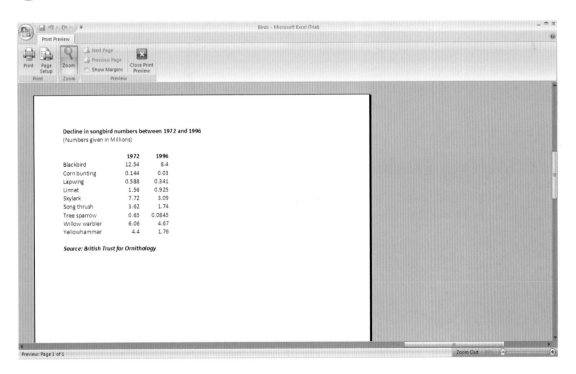

Figure 7.8

Only the selected cells appear in the print preview.

Click **Print**, then **OK** to print.

If you wanted to print the whole sheet again, you could either set the print area to include the chart, or you could click the **Print Area** button and select **Clear Print Area**.

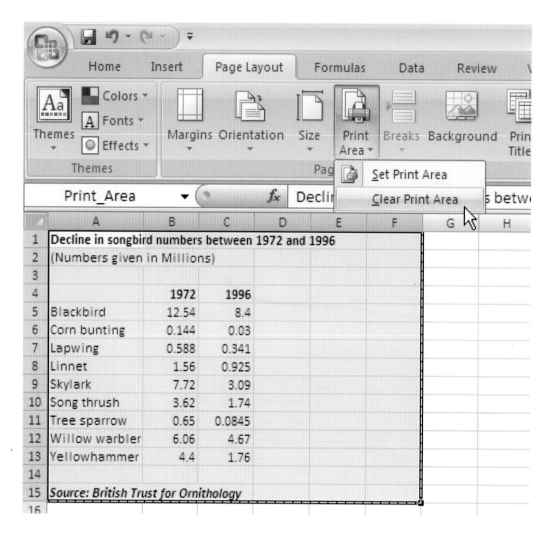

Figure 7.9

Printing row and column headings

Make sure **Sheet1** is selected and swap to the **Page Layout** tab. Click the **Print Titles** button.

In the **Page Setup** dialogue box, click to select the **Sheet** tab. Click the check box next to **Row and column headings** under the **Print** section.

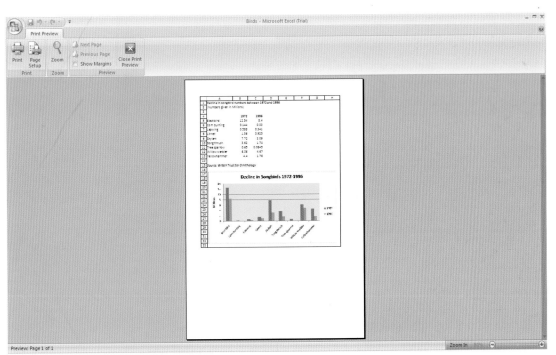

Figure 7.10

▶ Now click the **Print Preview** button in the **Page Setup** dialogue box (see Figure 7.10) to see what effect this has.

Tip:
You don't have to preview a page before you print it. You can go straight to the Print dialogue box by clicking the Office button and selecting Print and then Print from the menu.

Figure 7.11

▶ Close the **Print Preview** window by clicking the **Close** button.

Printing the title row on every page

Tip:
For some reason, if you enter the Page Setup dialogue box from Print Preview, the option to repeat the title row is deactivated. Make sure you enter Page Setup from the Print Titles button instead.

If you have a very large worksheet that spans two or three pages, it is useful to have the title repeated on pages 2 and 3. You can do this in the **Page Setup** dialogue box.

▶ First we'll set the print area to run onto more than one page. Select cell **A1** and drag down to cell **K80** or so.

▶ Swap to the **Page Layout** tab, click the **Print Area** button and select the **Set Print Area** option.

▶ Click the **Office Button** and go to **Print Preview**. The document is now **four** pages long – **two** pages wide and **two** down. Close the **Print Preview** window.

▶ Click the **Print Titles** button on the **Page Layout** tab on the **Ribbon** to open the **Page Setup** dialogue box.

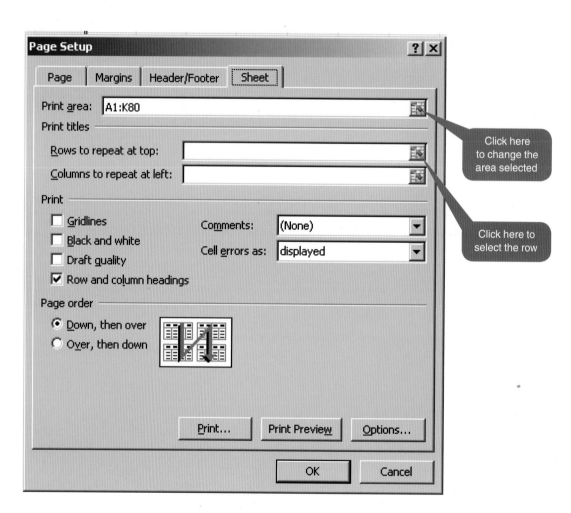

Figure 7.12

Here you can either:

 type **$1:$1** to select row **1** as the title row, or

 select the cells by clicking the icon on the right of the box. The cursor will become a small horizontal arrow, with which you should point and click row **1**.

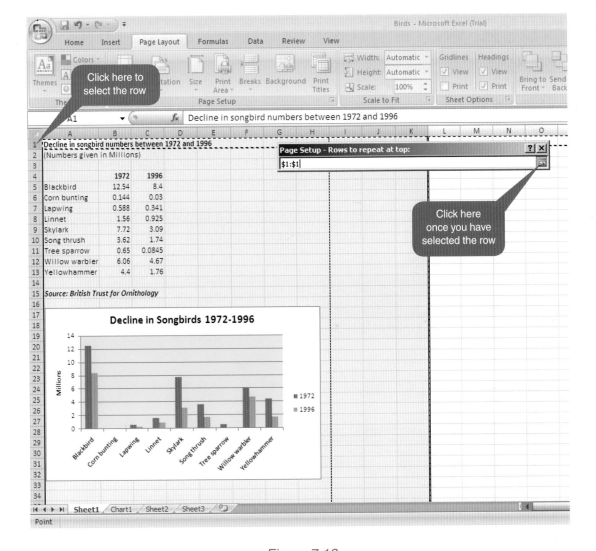

Figure 7.13

▶ When you have selected row **1**, click the small icon in the right of the box (see Figure 7.13).

▶ You also have the option of repeating a column, which you do in exactly the same way as rows. Try repeating column **A**, using the same method as for repeating row **1**.

▶ Click **Print Preview**.

It's not very neat (the cells may benefit from formatting) but the title row and column are repeated. Note that the title row and column will only appear on two of the four sheets. If we'd chosen a print area that was four pages long but only one page wide, the title row would appear on every sheet. To move from page to page in **Print Preview**, you use the scroll bar on the right of the screen.

▶ Either click **Print** and **OK**, or just close the **Print Preview** by clicking the **Close** button.

Fitting worksheet contents on one page

Although we've selected a print area that is larger than it needs to be, you are likely to come across spreadsheets that have enough data to fill more than one page. In this case, it is sometimes convenient to try and fit all the data onto one page for printing purposes.

 Check that **A1** to **K80** are still selected.

 Click the **Print Titles** button on the **Page Layout** tab on the **Ribbon** to open the **Page Setup** dialogue box as before.

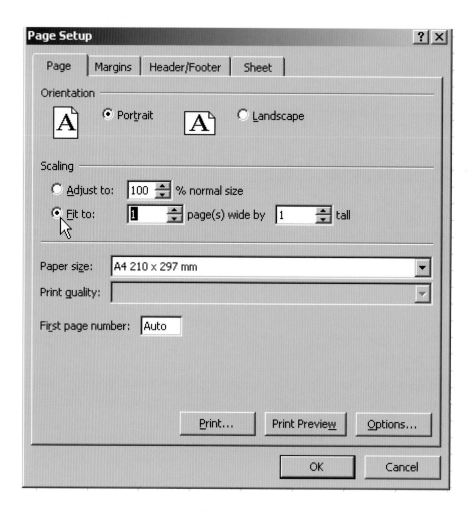

Figure 7.14

▶ Check that the **Print area** in the **Sheet** tab is **A1:K80** and then swap to the **Page** tab.

▶ Notice the option **Fit to:** under the **Scaling** section. Click the radio button on its left, and leave the other options as **1 page wide by 1 page tall**.

▶ Click **Print Preview**.

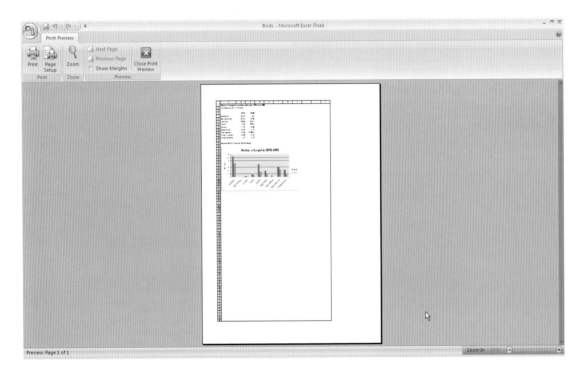

Figure 7.15

The cell range is the same as before, but now there is only one page, instead of four.

▶ Click **Close** to close the **Print Preview** window.

Other Page Setup options

Hiding/Unhiding gridlines on printouts

Excel automatically prints without gridlines, but sometimes they can be useful.

▶ Click **Sheet1** to select it.

▶ Open the **Page Setup** dialogue box as before.

Tip:
You can also open the Page Setup dialogue box by clicking the Setup button when you're in Print Preview.

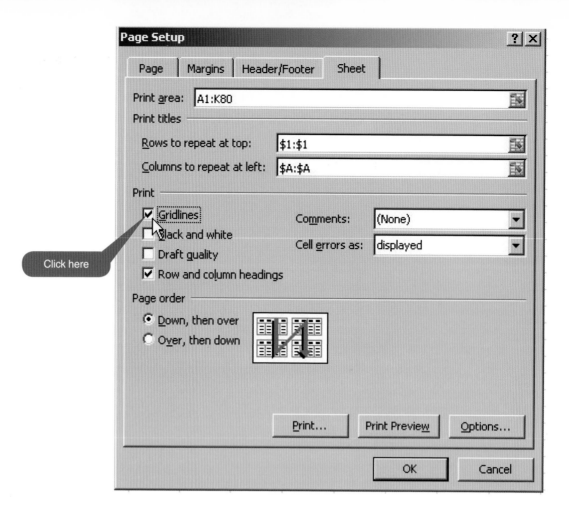

Figure 7.16

▶ Under the **Print** section, notice there is a check box next to **Gridlines**. Click this to print gridlines.

▶ Now go to **Print Preview** to see what it will look like.

Paper Orientation

▶ In the **Page Setup** dialogue box, click the **Page** tab.

▶ Click the buttons to change the orientation from **Portrait** to **Landscape** (see Figure 7.17).

Paper Size

 To change the paper size, click the down-arrow on the right of the box and select the correct paper size (see Figure 7.17).

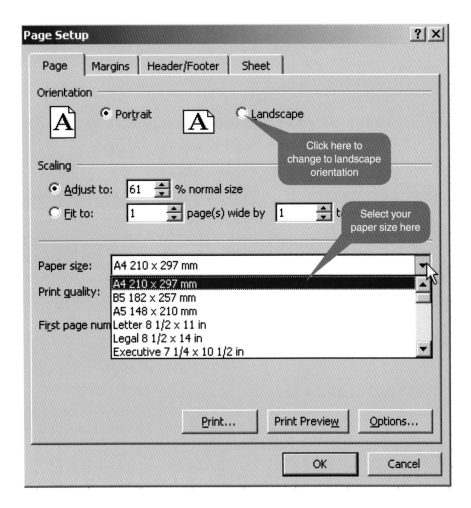

Figure 7.17

Changing the margins

 This is also done in **Page Setup**. Just click the **Margins** tab and choose which margin sizes you want.

 Click **OK** to close the **Page Setup** dialogue box.

There are two different ways of referencing a particular cell in a formula: relative and absolute cell referencing.

Relative cell referencing

This is the default setting in Excel. If we take the example in the screenshot below, Excel actually remembers the formula as **=the cell 3 above and one to the left**. This means that when you copy the formula to a different cell, the formula will no longer say **=A1**.

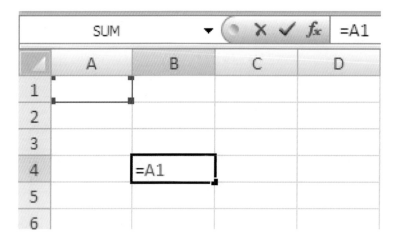

Figure 8.1

For example, if you copy cell **B4** to cell **C4**, the formula becomes **=B1**, because **B1** is the cell **3** above and one to the left of cell **C4**!

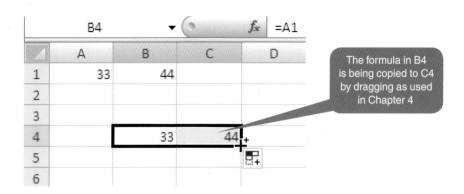

The formula in B4 is being copied to C4 by dragging as used in Chapter 4

Figure 8.2

 Create a spreadsheet like the one above and have a play with copying and pasting cells and formulas.

▶ Close the spreadsheet when you have finished. There is no need to save it.

Absolute cell referencing

Absolute cell referencing is used when you always want to refer to the same cell. We'll work through the project below to demonstrate when to use absolute cell referencing.

Project: Car imports

▶ Open a new workbook. Copy the spreadsheet shown in Figure 8.3, entering all the cell contents and copying the formatting.

	A	B	C	D	E	F	
1							
2	Current exchange rate:	1.55	Euros to the pound				
3							
4							
5		UK Price	Imported Price				
6	Car make & model	Price in Pounds	Price in Euros	Price in Pounds	£ Saving	% Saving	
7	Peugeot 206 Coupe Cabriolet	15370	20723.5				
8	VW Golf GTI	18330	24792.25				
9	Mini 16V Cooper	15465	21583.75				
10	BMW 5 Series SE	33060	44942.25				
11	VW Passat SE	17120	21692.25				
12	Alfa Romeo T Spark Selespeed Lusso	18750	24025				
13	Toyota Yaris 16V	11470	13942.25				
14							
15							

Book2

Sheet1 / Sheet2 / Sheet3

Figure 8.3

Tip:
The text has been right-aligned so that it lines up with the numbers below. To do this, highlight the text cells and click the **Align Right** button on the **Formatting** toolbar.

First we need to enter a formula to calculate the price of the imported cars in Pounds. The price will be calculated using the current exchange rate which is entered at the top of the sheet.

▶ Click in cell **D7**. Enter the formula **=C7/B2**. (To convert Euros to Pounds, you need to divide the Euro amount by the exchange rate.) Press **Enter**.

We need the same formula in all the cells in that column, from **D7** to **D13**. Let's see what happens when we copy the formula down.

▶ Click in cell **D7**. Click and drag the small handle on the bottom right of the cell down to cell **D13**.

Imported Price		
Price in Euros	Price in Pounds	£ Saving
20723.5	13370	Click and drag this handle
24792.25		

Figure 8.4

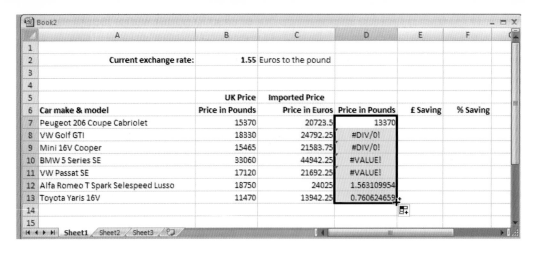

Figure 8.5

Excel has automatically used relative cell referencing, and as you can see, it hasn't worked!

 Click cell **D8** to see what formula is there.

The **Formula** bar shows **=C8/B3**. What is in cell **B3**? Nothing! Take a look at the other formulas in the column. Can you see what has happened?

We should have used absolute cell referencing, as we always want the formula to refer to cell **B2** where the exchange rate is.

 Select cells **D8** to **D13** and press the **Delete** key.

 Click in cell **D7**. We need to alter the formula to make **B2** an absolute cell reference.

For absolute cell referencing, all you do is add a **$** symbol in front of the column AND row. You can put the symbol in front of the column only, but this will mean that when you copy the formula, only the column part of the formula will be kept constant. The same goes for rows.

 Change the formula in cell **D7** to **=C7/$B$2**.

Figure 8.6

 Now copy the formula to the other cells in the column.

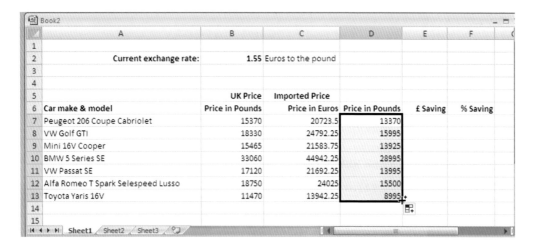

Figure 8.7

That seems to have worked!

▶ Save the worksheet as **Cars** by clicking the **Office** button, selecting **Save As** and the **Excel Workbook** option.

Entering the other formulas

▶ You need to enter a formula for the **£ Saving** column. For this, use the formula **UK Price in Pounds – Imported Price in Pounds**.

UK Price	Imported Price		£ Saving
Price in Pounds	Price in Euros	Price in Pounds	
15370	20723.5	13370	=B7-D7

Figure 8.8

▶ Copy the formula down the whole column. Do you need relative or absolute cell referencing for this?

Your spreadsheet should look like the one in Figure 8.9 – check your formulas if you're getting different figures.

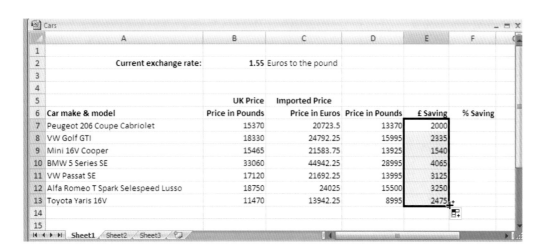

Figure 8.9

Calculating a percentage

We also need a formula for the % **Saving** column.

▶ Enter the formula for this calculation in cell **F7**: **£Saving/UK Price in Pounds**.

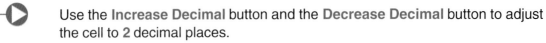

UK Price	Imported Price			
Price in Pounds	Price in Euros	Price in Pounds	£ Saving	% Saving
15370	20723.5	13370	2000	=E7/B7

Figure 8.10

It might look like the answer is 0 – this is because there are no decimal places shown.

▶ Use the **Increase Decimal** button and the **Decrease Decimal** button to adjust the cell to **2** decimal places.

▶ Copy the formula down for all the cars.

▶ To turn them into percentages, select cells **F7** to **F13** then click the **Percent** button on the **Home** tab on the **Ribbon**.

Figure 8.11

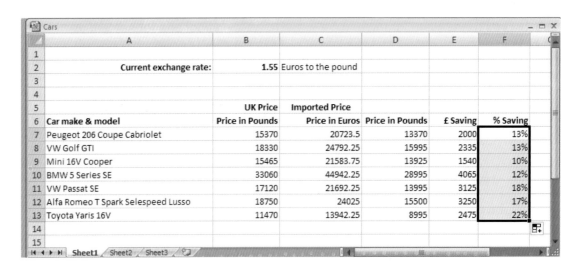

	A	B	C	D	E	F
1						
2	Current exchange rate:	1.55	Euros to the pound			
3						
4						
5		UK Price	Imported Price			
6	Car make & model	Price in Pounds	Price in Euros	Price in Pounds	£ Saving	% Saving
7	Peugeot 206 Coupe Cabriolet	15370	20723.5	13370	2000	13%
8	VW Golf GTI	18330	24792.25	15995	2335	13%
9	Mini 16V Cooper	15465	21583.75	13925	1540	10%
10	BMW 5 Series SE	33060	44942.25	28995	4065	12%
11	VW Passat SE	17120	21692.25	13995	3125	18%
12	Alfa Romeo T Spark Selespeed Lusso	18750	24025	15500	3250	17%
13	Toyota Yaris 16V	11470	13942.25	8995	2475	22%
14						
15						

Figure 8.12

▶ Have a play with the exchange rate. At what exchange rate does the % **Saving** become zero for the Mini?

The currency format

Now we'll change the format of some of the columns to give them the **Currency** number type.

 Select cells **B7** to **B13**, then hold down **Ctrl** while selecting cells **D7** to **E13**.

 Right click anywhere within the selected cells to bring up the shortcut menu.

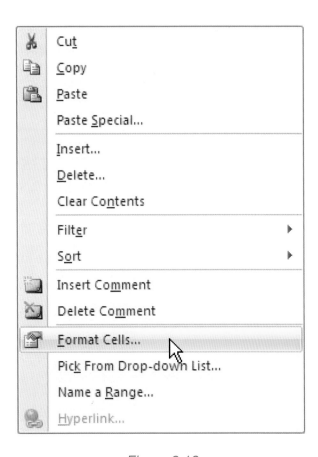

Figure 8.13

 Select **Format Cells** from the menu.

 Make sure the **Number** tab is selected and then select **Currency** from the **Category** list. Set the **Decimal places** to **0**. Excel should choose the £ symbol by default, which is fine.

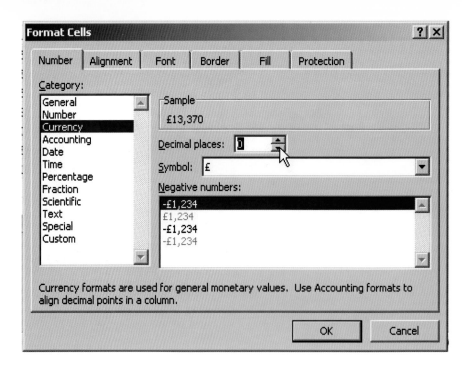

Figure 8.14

 Click **OK**.

 Repeat this for the **Euro** column. Remember to choose the **Euro** symbol from the **Symbol** list.

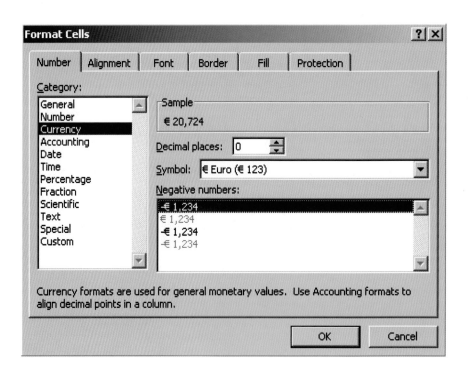

Figure 8.15

Your spreadsheet should now look like the one in Figure 8.16.

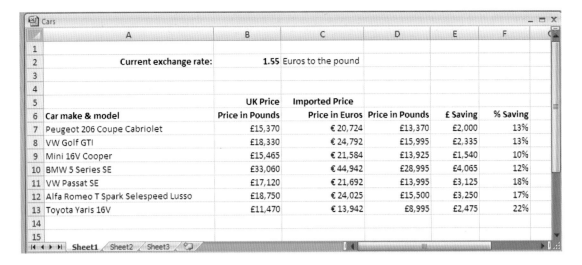

	A	B	C	D	E	F
1						
2	Current exchange rate:	1.55	Euros to the pound			
3						
4						
5		UK Price	Imported Price			
6	Car make & model	Price in Pounds	Price in Euros	Price in Pounds	£ Saving	% Saving
7	Peugeot 206 Coupe Cabriolet	£15,370	€ 20,724	£13,370	£2,000	13%
8	VW Golf GTI	£18,330	€ 24,792	£15,995	£2,335	13%
9	Mini 16V Cooper	£15,465	€ 21,584	£13,925	£1,540	10%
10	BMW 5 Series SE	£33,060	€ 44,942	£28,995	£4,065	12%
11	VW Passat SE	£17,120	€ 21,692	£13,995	£3,125	18%
12	Alfa Romeo T Spark Selespeed Lusso	£18,750	€ 24,025	£15,500	£3,250	17%
13	Toyota Yaris 16V	£11,470	€ 13,942	£8,995	£2,475	22%
14						
15						

Figure 8.16

Merge and centre cell contents

You can easily merge and centre cell contents using the button on the **Formatting** toolbar. This is particularly useful for titles.

▶ Select cells **C5** and **D5**. Click the **Merge and Centre** button.

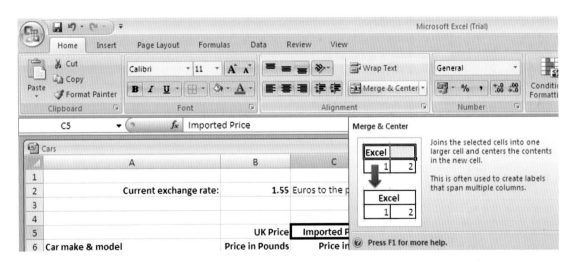

Figure 8.17

Doing this makes it a bit easier to see which of the prices are imported.

Adding a date field

We will add a date to show when the **Current exchange rate** was last updated.

▶ Type **Updated:** in cell **D2** as shown below in Figure 8.18.

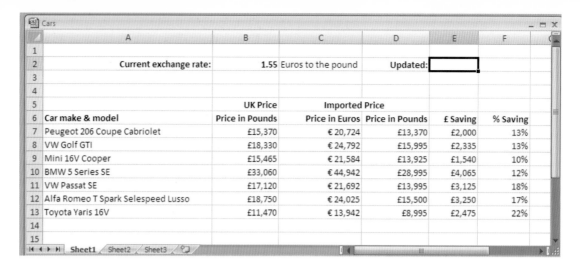

	A	B	C	D	E	F
1						
2	Current exchange rate:	1.55	Euros to the pound	Updated:		
3						
4						
5		UK Price	Imported Price			
6	Car make & model	Price in Pounds	Price in Euros	Price in Pounds	£ Saving	% Saving
7	Peugeot 206 Coupe Cabriolet	£15,370	€ 20,724	£13,370	£2,000	13%
8	VW Golf GTI	£18,330	€ 24,792	£15,995	£2,335	13%
9	Mini 16V Cooper	£15,465	€ 21,584	£13,925	£1,540	10%
10	BMW 5 Series SE	£33,060	€ 44,942	£28,995	£4,065	12%
11	VW Passat SE	£17,120	€ 21,692	£13,995	£3,125	18%
12	Alfa Romeo T Spark Selespeed Lusso	£18,750	€ 24,025	£15,500	£3,250	17%
13	Toyota Yaris 16V	£11,470	€ 13,942	£8,995	£2,475	22%
14						
15						

Figure 8.18

▶ Type the date (as numbers, set out as DD/MM/YY) in cell **E2**, press **Enter** and then right click in the cell. Select **Format Cells** from the shortcut menu that appears.

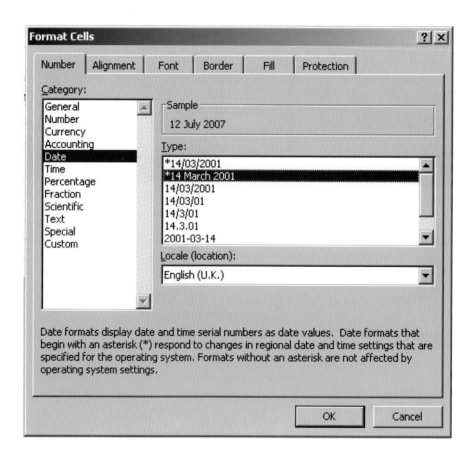

Figure 8.19

▶ Excel has already guessed that you want the **Date** category. Pick a date **Type** from the right-hand list. This only selects a format for the date display, not the actual date. Note that although it looks like Excel has the day and month mixed up, it will get it right when you click **OK**.

▶ You might need to widen column **E** to display the whole date.

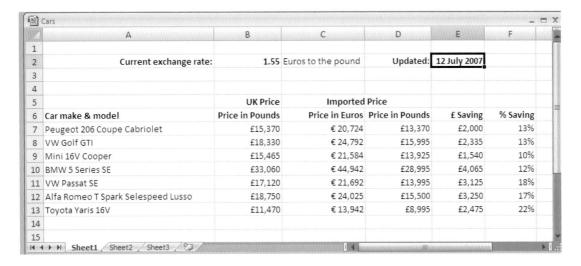

Cars						
	A	B	C	D	E	F
1						
2	Current exchange rate:	1.55	Euros to the pound	Updated:	12 July 2007	
3						
4						
5		UK Price	Imported Price			
6	Car make & model	Price in Pounds	Price in Euros	Price in Pounds	£ Saving	% Saving
7	Peugeot 206 Coupe Cabriolet	£15,370	€ 20,724	£13,370	£2,000	13%
8	VW Golf GTI	£18,330	€ 24,792	£15,995	£2,335	13%
9	Mini 16V Cooper	£15,465	€ 21,584	£13,925	£1,540	10%
10	BMW 5 Series SE	£33,060	€ 44,942	£28,995	£4,065	12%
11	VW Passat SE	£17,120	€ 21,692	£13,995	£3,125	18%
12	Alfa Romeo T Spark Selespeed Lusso	£18,750	€ 24,025	£15,500	£3,250	17%
13	Toyota Yaris 16V	£11,470	€ 13,942	£8,995	£2,475	22%
14						
15						

Figure 8.20

Wrapping cell content

Some of the entries under the heading **Car make & model** are quite long. It would look neater if the longer descriptions ran onto two lines, rather than making the column extra-wide to fit them.

▶ Select cell **A12**, then right click it. Select **Format Cells** from the shortcut menu that appears.

▶ The **Format Cells** dialogue box appears. Click the **Alignment** tab.

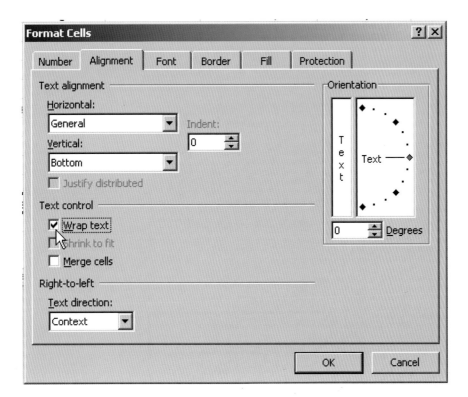

Figure 8.21

 Under the **Text Control** section, click the check box next to **Wrap text**. Click **OK**.

Now resize column **A** so that it is too small to fit all the words on one line.

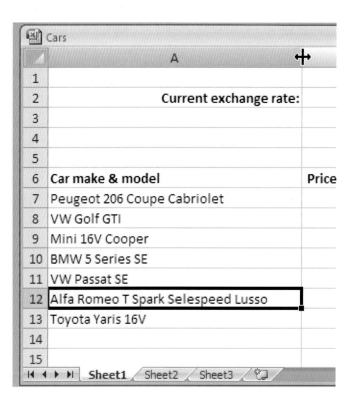

Figure 8.22

Widen row **12** by clicking and dragging between the row headers of row **12** and row **13**. An alternative is to double click between rows **12** and **13**.

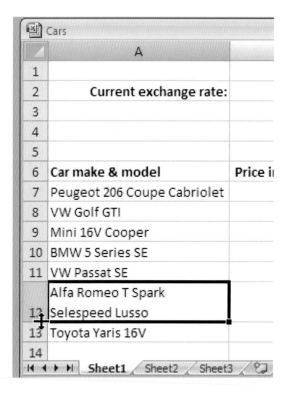

Figure 8.23

90

The text just fills onto the next line!

 Repeat this for some of the other cells where the **Car make & model** description is long.

 Now make the column headings in row **6** wrap over two lines.

 We need to move the **Updated** field over to the right. Select cells **D2** and **E2**, then click and drag the border of the selection to the right.

	A	B	C	D	E	F	G	H	I	J
1										
2	Current exchange rate:	1.55	Euros to the pound		Updated:	12 July 2007				
3										
4										
5		UK Price	Imported Price							
6	Car make & model	Price in Pounds	Price in Euros	Price in Pounds	£ Saving	% Saving				
7	Peugeot 206 Coupe Cabriolet	£15,370	€ 20,724	£13,370	£2,000	13%				
8	VW Golf GTI	£18,330	€ 24,792	£15,995	£2,335	13%				
9	Mini 16V Cooper	£15,465	€ 21,584	£13,925	£1,540	10%				
10	BMW 5 Series SE	£33,060	€ 44,942	£28,995	£4,065	12%				
11	VW Passat SE	£17,120	€ 21,692	£13,995	£3,125	18%				
12	Alfa Romeo T Spark Selespeed Lusso	£18,750	€ 24,025	£15,500	£3,250	17%				
13	Toyota Yaris 16V	£11,470	€ 13,942	£8,995	£2,475	22%				
14										

Figure 8.24

Adding borders

We'll just quickly add some borders to make the headings a little clearer.

 Select cells **B5** and **B6**. Click the small down-arrow on the **Borders** icon on the **Home** tab on the **Ribbon**.

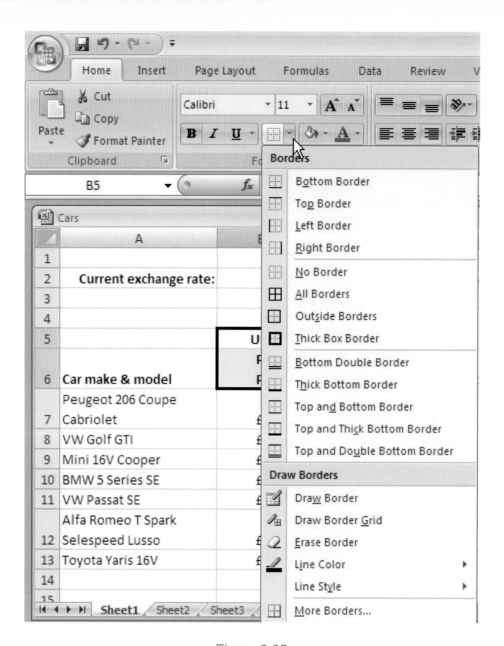

Figure 8.25

There are lots of different types of borders to choose from. Select the one shown.

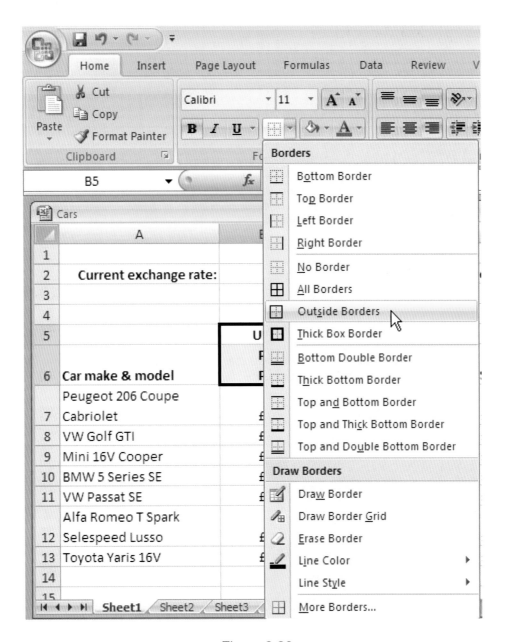

Figure 8.26

▶ Now select cells **C5** to **D6**. You don't need to click the down-arrow this time, just click the middle of the **Borders** icon. It will automatically create the same sort of border as before.

▶ Repeat this for the various groups of cells, until your spreadsheet looks something like the one shown in Figure 8.27.

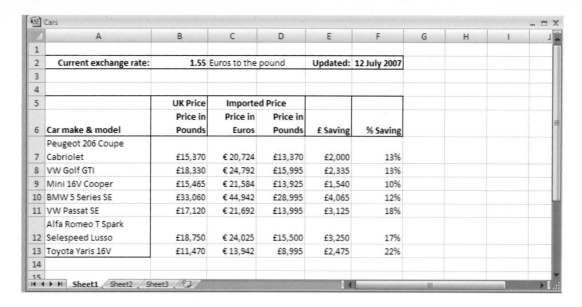

Tip:
To delete a border, just click the cell next to the border, and click the No Border option from the Borders menu.

Figure 8.27

▶ Finally, draw one big border around the table, using the slightly thicker border.

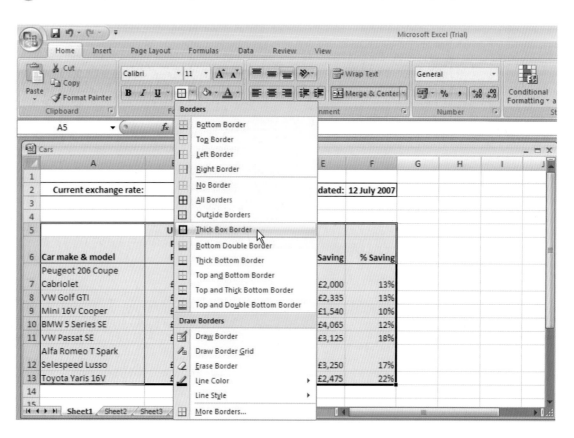

Figure 8.28

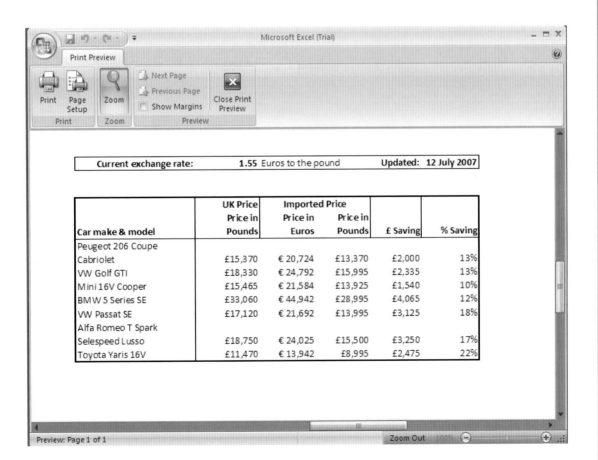

Cars									
	A	B	C	D	E	F	G	H	I
1									
2	Current exchange rate:	1.55	Euros to the pound		Updated: 12 July 2007				
3									
4									
5		UK Price	Imported Price						
6	Car make & model	Price in Pounds	Price in Euros	Price in Pounds	£ Saving	% Saving			
7	Peugeot 206 Coupe Cabriolet	£15,370	€ 20,724	£13,370	£2,000	13%			
8	VW Golf GTI	£18,330	€ 24,792	£15,995	£2,335	13%			
9	Mini 16V Cooper	£15,465	€ 21,584	£13,925	£1,540	10%			
10	BMW 5 Series SE	£33,060	€ 44,942	£28,995	£4,065	12%			
11	VW Passat SE	£17,120	€ 21,692	£13,995	£3,125	18%			
12	Alfa Romeo T Spark Selespeed Lusso	£18,750	€ 24,025	£15,500	£3,250	17%			
13	Toyota Yaris 16V	£11,470	€ 13,942	£8,995	£2,475	22%			
14									

Sheet1 / Sheet2 / Sheet3

Figure 8.29

Click the **Office** button and then **Print** and **Print Preview** to see what your spreadsheet will look like when printed. You may need to change the **Page Orientation** to **Landscape** for it all to fit on one page.

Tip:
You can change the Page Orientation in Print Preview by clicking the Page Setup button and then selecting Landscape in the Page Setup dialogue box.

Figure 8.30

Click **Close** to exit **Print Preview**.

Find and replace

There aren't many records in this spreadsheet, but in larger spreadsheets it is useful to be able to search for a particular value.

Finding a cell containing a particular word or value

▶ On the **Home** tab, click the **Find & Select** button and select **Find**.

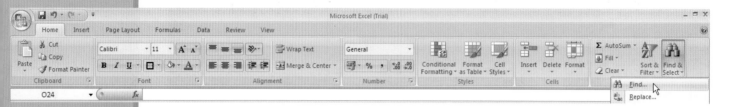

Figure 8.31

▶ The **Find and Replace** dialogue box opens:

▶ In the **Find** tab Enter **VW** in the **Find what:** box.

Figure 8.32

▶ Click **Find Next**.

▶ Excel makes the cell containing **VW** the active cell. Click **Find Next** again.

Excel moves to the second cell containing **VW**.

Replacing a word or value

If you have spelt a name wrongly in several different places in a spreadsheet, it is useful to set Excel to find and replace each instance of the word. For practice, we'll replace the word **VW** with **Volkswagen**.

▶ Click the **Replace** tab at the top of the **Find and Replace** dialogue box.

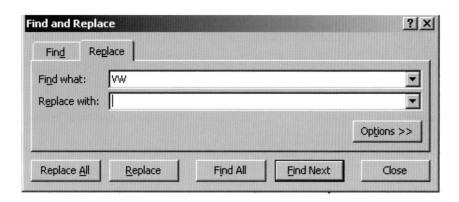

Figure 8.33

▶ Type **Volkswagen** in the **Replace with:** box.

▶ Click the **Replace All** button.

Figure 8.34

▶ Click **OK**. Notice that both instances of **VW** have now become **Volkswagen**. Click **Close**.

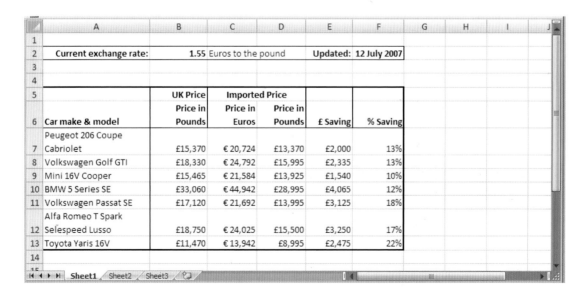

	A	B	C	D	E	F	G	H	I	J
1										
2	Current exchange rate:	1.55	Euros to the pound		Updated:	12 July 2007				
3										
4										
5		UK Price	Imported Price							
6	Car make & model	Price in Pounds	Price in Euros	Price in Pounds	£ Saving	% Saving				
7	Peugeot 206 Coupe Cabriolet	£15,370	€ 20,724	£13,370	£2,000	13%				
8	Volkswagen Golf GTI	£18,330	€ 24,792	£15,995	£2,335	13%				
9	Mini 16V Cooper	£15,465	€ 21,584	£13,925	£1,540	10%				
10	BMW 5 Series SE	£33,060	€ 44,942	£28,995	£4,065	12%				
11	Volkswagen Passat SE	£17,120	€ 21,692	£13,995	£3,125	18%				
12	Alfa Romeo T Spark Selespeed Lusso	£18,750	€ 24,025	£15,500	£3,250	17%				
13	Toyota Yaris 16V	£11,470	€ 13,942	£8,995	£2,475	22%				
14										

Sheet1 / Sheet2 / Sheet3

Figure 8.35

Adding headers and footers

Headers and footers are useful for automatically inserting information such as the current date and page numbers on larger documents.

▶ Swap to the **Insert** tab on the **Ribbon** and click the **Header & Footer** button.

▶ The **Header & Footer Tools** tab becomes active, showing the **Design** tab.

Tip:
You can also view the Header and Footer options in the Page Setup dialogue box. To do this, swap to the Page Layout tab and click the Print Titles button.

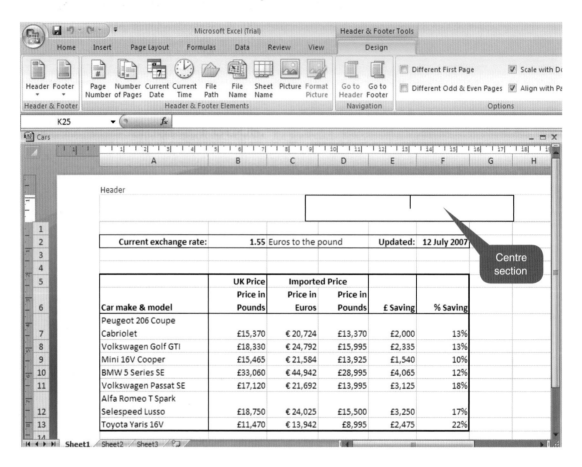

Figure 8.36

▶ Click in the **Center Section** box and type **Car Import Savings Sheet**.

This title text should be bold; we'll do this now.

▶ Highlight the text you have just typed then click the **Font** button, which initially appears as a ghostly image above the highlighted text – see Figure 8.37:

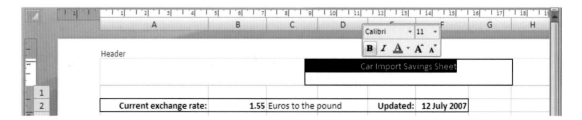

Figure 8.37

▶ Make the text **12** point and bold.

▶ Click away from the text to remove the highlight and view the results.

Now we'll insert some fields into the **Footer**.

▶ Click in the **Header** area, which opens the **Header & Footer Tools** tab showing the **Design** tab. Click the **Go to Footer** button. An alternative way of getting to it is to scroll to the bottom of the page, where the footer is obvious, and click in the **Footer** area which makes it active and enables you to make changes.

What do all the buttons do?

There are quite a few buttons to choose from!

▶ To find out what a button does, hover the mouse pointer over a button for a few seconds. A small box pops up telling you what the button does.

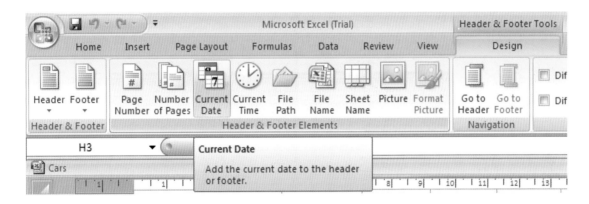

Figure 8.38

Inserting the filename

▶ Click somewhere in the **Left Section** box at the top of the worksheet.

▶ Click the **Filename** button.

Inserting the worksheet name

▶ Type a comma and a space after the **Filename** expression then click the **Sheet Name** button on the **Header & Footer Tools** tab.

Inserting the page number

This is only really useful in longer documents, but we'll add it anyway for practice.

▶ Click in the **Center Section** at the top of the worksheet (see Figure 8.36). Click the **Page Number** button.

Inserting the date

▶ Click in the **Right Section** at the top of the worksheet, then click the **Current Date** button.

Inserting the time

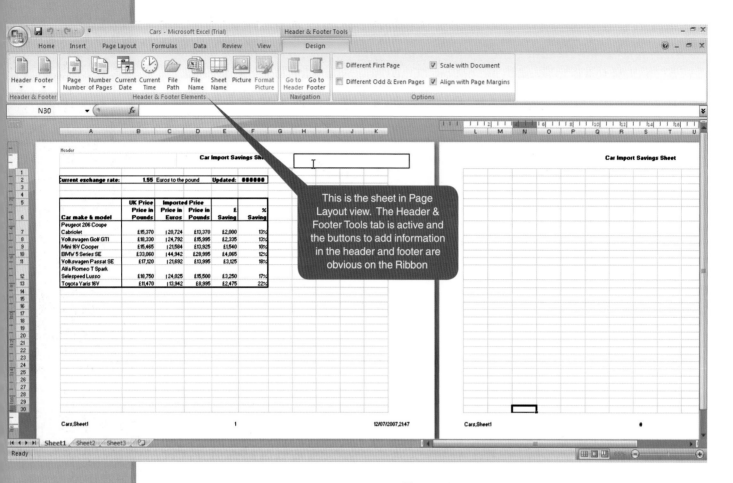

> Type a comma and a space after the date then click the **Current Time** button on the **Header & Footer Tools** tab.

This is the sheet in Page Layout view. The Header & Footer Tools tab is active and the buttons to add information in the header and footer are obvious on the Ribbon

Figure 8.39

Clicking in the body of the sheet will enable you to see the results of the changes that you have just made. While you are making changes and additions to the header and footer, you will have noticed that the layout has changed; this is called **Page Layout** view and it is a useful way of viewing what the printed sheet will look like. If you wish to return to the original view, click in the body of the sheet, swap to the **View** tab and click the **Normal** button at the left-hand side of the **Ribbon**. This will result in your header and footer disappearing from your screen, but they still remain, even though they're no longer visible, as can be seen if you look at the sheet in **Print Preview** (click on the **Office** button and then **Print** to get to it).

> Click **Print Preview** to see what the sheet will look like when printed.

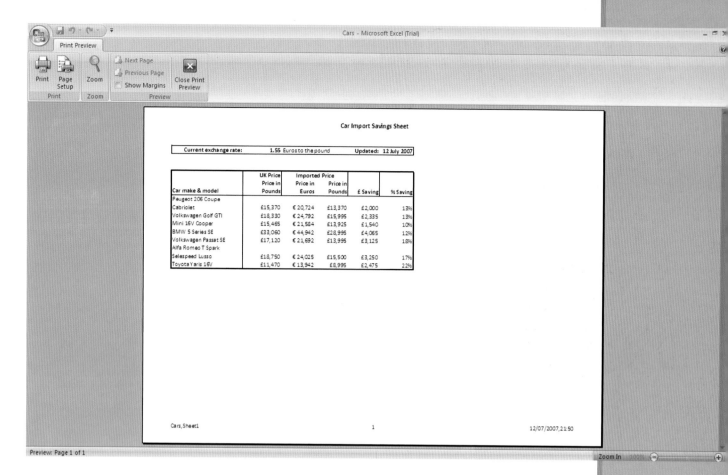

Print Preview

Print | Page Setup | Zoom | Next Page | Previous Page | Show Margins | Close Print Preview

Print | Zoom | Preview

Car Import Savings Sheet

| Current exchange rate: | 1.55 Euros to the pound | | Updated: | 12 July 2007 |

Car make & model	UK Price Price in Pounds	Imported Price Price in Euros	Price in Pounds	£ Saving	% Saving
Peugeot 206 Coupe Cabriolet	£15,370	€ 20,724	£13,370	£2,000	13%
Volkswagen Golf GTI	£18,330	€ 24,792	£15,995	£2,335	13%
Mini 16V Cooper	£15,465	€ 21,584	£13,925	£1,540	10%
BMW 5 Series SE	£33,060	€ 44,942	£28,995	£4,065	12%
Volkswagen Passat SE	£17,120	€ 21,692	£13,995	£3,125	18%
Alfa Romeo T Spark Selespeed Lusso	£18,750	€ 24,025	£15,500	£3,250	17%
Toyota Yaris 16V	£11,470	€ 13,942	£8,995	£2,475	22%

Cars,Sheet1

1

12/07/2007,21:50

Preview: Page 1 of 1

Zoom In

Figure 8.40

 Print the spreadsheet if you like, otherwise click the **Close** button.

 Save and close the spreadsheet.

Chapter 9 – IF ... THEN ... ELSE ...

In this chapter we'll create a spreadsheet for a mirror shop. The shop offers cut-to-size mirrors, and they need a spreadsheet that will give an instant quote for a customer, given the required size.

Project: Create a spreadsheet to produce instant quotes

The shop offers only one thickness of glass, 6mm. It offers a choice of polished, or polished and bevelled edges.

The price of the mirror is dependent on the surface area and the perimeter length.

These are the prices:

£32 per square metre of surface area

£1.70 per linear metre of perimeter for polished edges

£2.10 per linear metre of perimeter for polished and bevelled edges.

 Open a new workbook and type in the text then format it and add borders so that your spreadsheet looks like Figure 9.1.

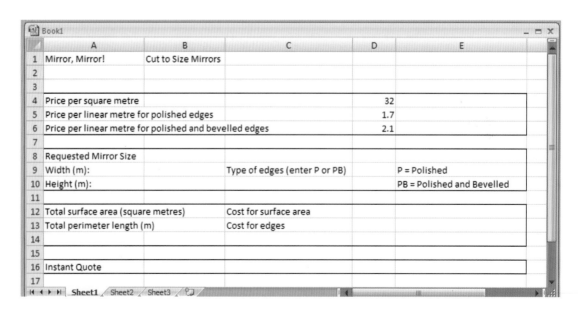

	A	B	C	D	E
1	Mirror, Mirror!	Cut to Size Mirrors			
2					
3					
4	Price per square metre			32	
5	Price per linear metre for polished edges			1.7	
6	Price per linear metre for polished and bevelled edges			2.1	
7					
8	Requested Mirror Size				
9	Width (m):		Type of edges (enter P or PB)	P = Polished	
10	Height (m):			PB = Polished and Bevelled	
11					
12	Total surface area (square metres)	Cost for surface area			
13	Total perimeter length (m)	Cost for edges			
14					
15					
16	Instant Quote				
17					

Figure 9.1

Changing font style and size

We need to give the title and some of the other headings a bit of a makeover.

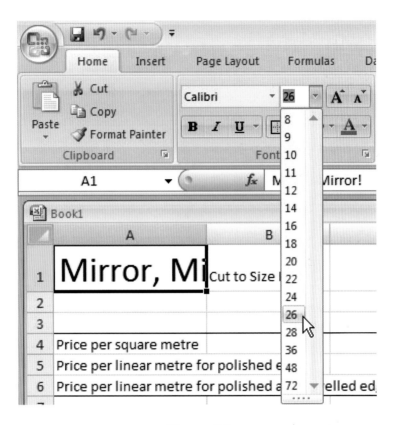

▶ Select cell **A1** and use the controls in the **Font** group of the **Home** tab to select size **26** font.

Figure 9.2

▶ Now change the font. Choose any font you like the look of. Make it bold by clicking the **Bold** icon.

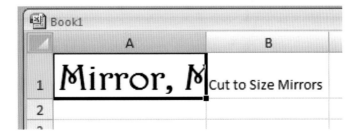

Figure 9.3

▶ You need to move the contents of cell **B1** to cell **D1**. Make sure cell **B1** is selected, then click and drag the black border over to cell **D1**.

▶ Change some more of the headings' formatting options to make your spreadsheet look like Figure 9.4.

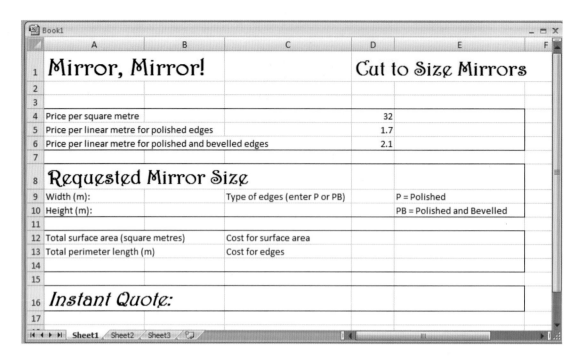

Figure 9.4

Adding the formulas

We'll do some more formatting in a minute. First we have to enter the formulas.

▶ The calculation for **Total surface area** is **Width × Height**. Enter the formula in cell **B12** as **=B9*B10**.

▶ The calculation for **Total perimeter length** is **2 × (Width + Height)**. Enter the formula as **=2*(B9+B10)**. You will need the brackets in the formula.

▶ Enter the formula for **Cost for surface area**. It should be **=B12*D4**.

▶ Save the workbook as **Mirrors**.

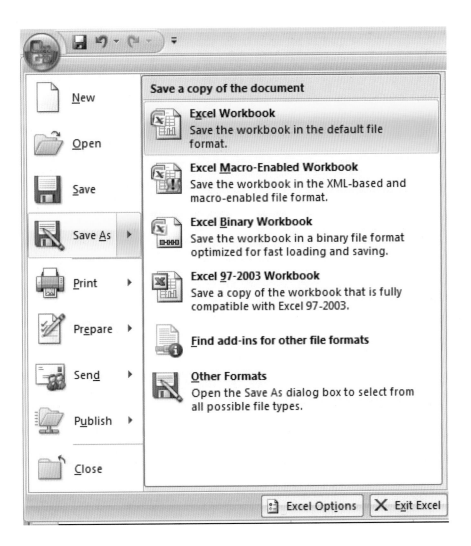

Figure 9.5

Enter some data

▶ Try out your formulas by entering the width and height of a mirror.

▶ Enter either **P** or **PB** where specified.

IF statements

Our calculation for the **Cost for edges** has to include an **IF** statement, so it can calculate the cost for either **Polished** or **Polished and Bevelled** edges.

IF edges are **Polished** THEN **Cost for edges** = **Total perimeter length (m)** *D5

IF edges are **Polished and Bevelled** THEN **Cost for edges** = **Total perimeter length (m)** *D6

Tip:
IF is a so-called 'Logical function'.

Breaking these statements down further:

IF cell **D9** = P THEN cell **D13** = B13*D5

IF cell **D9** = PB THEN cell **D13** = B13*D6

▶ Select cell **D13**. Click the **Insert Function** button just to the left of the Formula bar.

Figure 9.6

▶ In the **Insert Function** dialogue box, select **IF** from the list. If you cannot see it in the list, change the **category** box to **Logical**.

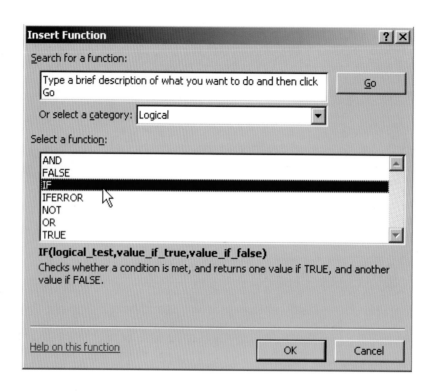

Figure 9.7

Tip:
If you're confused about how this function works, try clicking the Help on this function link at the bottom of the window. This gives an explanation and some more examples.

▶ Click **OK**.

▶ Enter the formulas in Figure 9.8 into the **Function Arguments** dialogue box.

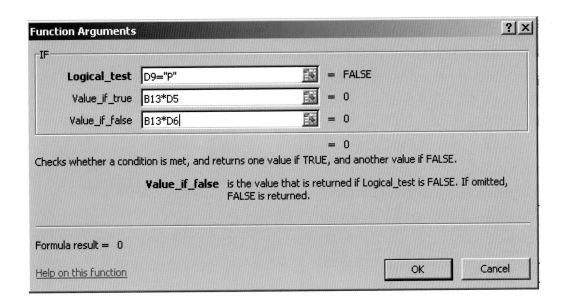

Figure 9.8

▶ Click **OK**.

▶ Format all the currency cells to show pound signs and have **2** decimal places, if you haven't done so already.

▶ Finally fill in the last formula for the total cost, next to the **Instant Quote** heading. It should be **=SUM(D12:D13)**.

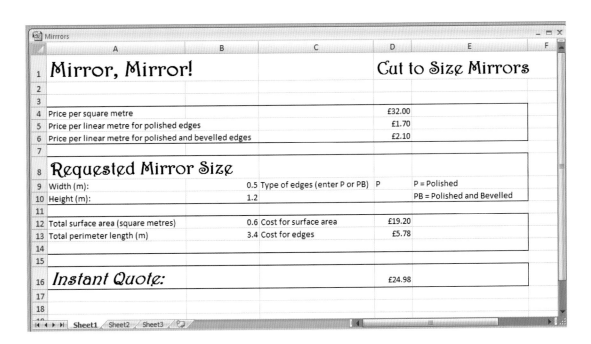

Figure 9.9

Adding some colour

It would be nice if the spreadsheet was a bit more colourful. We can do this by changing the font colour and the background fill colour.

Changing the font colour

▶ Select cell **A1**.

▶ Click the down-arrow on the **Font Color** button.

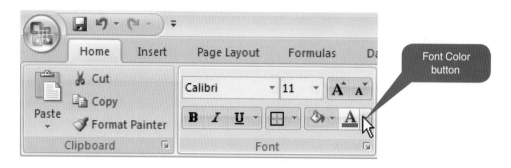

Figure 9.10

Figure 9.11

▶ Click any colour to select it.

Changing the background fill colour

▶ With cell **A1** still selected, click the down-arrow on the **Background Fill** button.

Figure 9.12

▶ Click to select a colour.

Aligning cell content

You can set where the text appears in a cell – left, right, top, bottom or centre.

▶ Widen row **1** by clicking and dragging between the row selectors of row **1** and row **2**.

▶ Select cells **A1** and **D1**. Right click somewhere in a selected cell.

▶ Select **Format Cells** from the menu.

▶ Click the **Alignment** tab. Select **Center** in the **Vertical Alignment** box. Take a look at the other alignment options – they might come in useful!

Tip:
You use the Format Cells dialogue box to change the alignment of the cells. You can make the text vertical if you like!

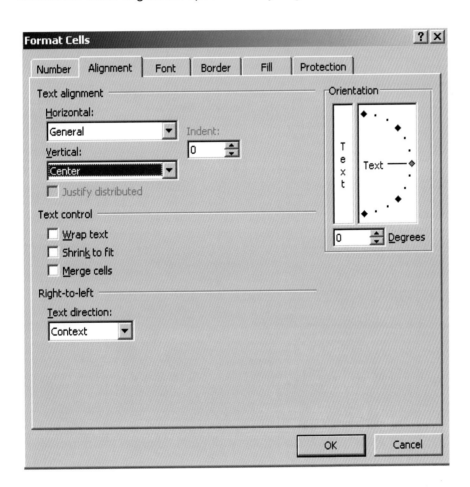

Figure 9.13

Cell orientation

You can change the orientation of the text in the cells using the **Format Cells** dialogue box.

▶ Click and drag the red dot so that the text is slightly diagonal.

Figure 9.14

▶ Click **OK**.

Add some more colours, and play around with the formatting so that your spreadsheet looks something like the one shown in Figure 9.15.

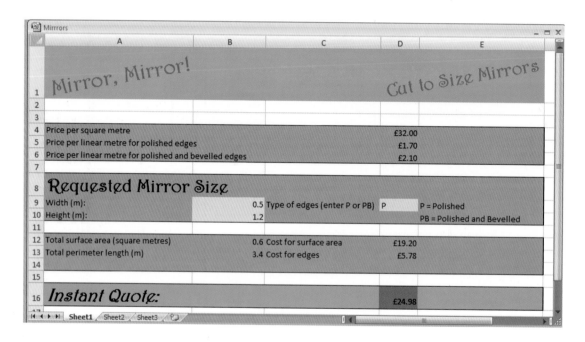

Figure 9.15

▶ Enter some different values for the width and height of the mirror. You can also change the prices.

▶ Save and close the spreadsheet when you're happy with it.

Chapter 10 – VLOOKUP

In this chapter we will create a spreadsheet that could be used by staff in ski rental shops. It will allow the staff to type in the customer's weight and ski level ability, and will then display the optimum ski length for them.

Project: Create a spreadsheet for a ski rental shop

Planning the spreadsheet

The first step is to find out what the ideal ski sizes are for skiers of various weights and abilities – any rental shop will probably have paper tables which they use to look up ski sizes. The aim of this spreadsheet is to computerise this paper chart to eliminate the need for staff to manually look up ski sizes.

The next step is to plan how the application will work. It must be quick and easy to use, so some thought needs to go into how the information is laid out and presented.

We will develop a simple version that will calculate ski lengths for beginners and intermediates only, and for just one type of ski. If you like, you can later develop the spreadsheet to include more options.

Building the spreadsheet

▶   Open a new workbook.

First we'll enter the recommended ski lengths for beginners.

▶ Type the heading **Ski Length Calculator** in cell **A1**.

▶ Centre the heading across cells **A1** to **D1** using the **Merge and Center** button. Have a play with the font size and style, and colour the cell to make the heading look a bit more interesting.

▶ Enter the rest of the data shown in Figure 10.1.

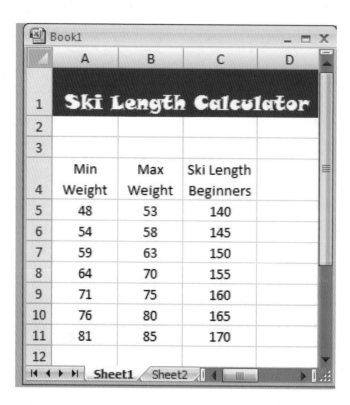

	A	B	C	D
1	Ski Length Calculator			
2				
3				
4	Min Weight	Max Weight	Ski Length Beginners	
5	48	53	140	
6	54	58	145	
7	59	63	150	
8	64	70	155	
9	71	75	160	
10	76	80	165	
11	81	85	170	
12				

Figure 10.1

Naming ranges

It is possible to rename individual cells and also cell ranges. Here we will name a cell range to make referring to the range much easier. By referring to named cells you will automatically be using absolute referencing.

▶ Highlight cells **A5** to **C11**.

▶ Swap to the **Formulas** tab and click the **Define Name** button in the **Defined Names** group.

▶ Name the selected range **SkiLength** and leave the **Scope** (the range of the workbook that will recognise this name) on **Workbook**. An entry in **Comment** is not necessary.

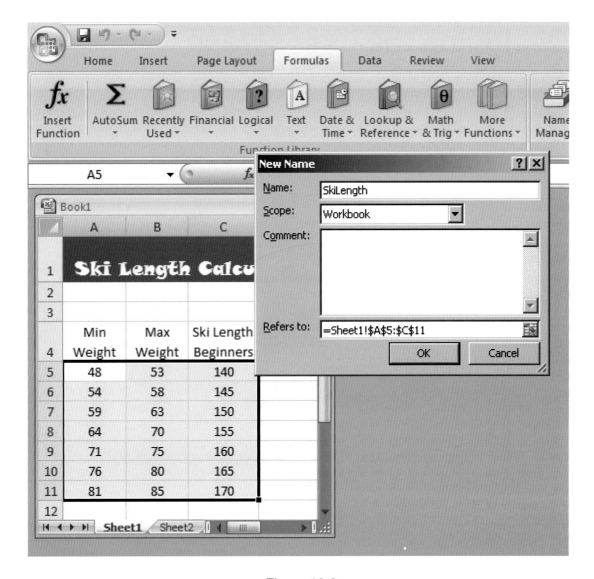

Figure 10.2

 Click **OK**.

Moving and renaming sheets

We need a main screen into which the customer's weight will need to be entered.

 Drag the sheet tab for **Sheet2** to the left of **Sheet1**.

 Right click the **Sheet2** tab and rename it **MainScreen**.

 Rename **Sheet1 SkiLengthChart**.

 Delete **Sheet3**.

Designing the user screen

Now we can display the screen that the ski shop staff will enter the data into, and which will display the correct length of ski for the customer.

▶ Click on the **MainScreen** sheet tab.

▶ Copy the design shown in Figure 10.3.

Figure 10.3

▶ Save your work as **SkiCalculator**.

Adding validation to cells

Validation is the checking of input data by software, to make sure that it is sensible or reasonable.

In this case, validation is used to make sure that when the customer weight is entered, it is within the allowed range. This reduces the chances of the user making an error when entering the weight.

▶ Click in cell **C3** on the **MainScreen** sheet.

▶ Select the **Data** tab and click the **Data Validation** button in the **Data Tools** group.

▶ In the **Data Validation** dialogue box, click the **Settings** tab and select **Whole number** from the first drop-down list. You are then asked for a data range. Enter **48** as the minimum weight in the **Minimum** box and **85** as the maximum weight in the **Maximum** box.

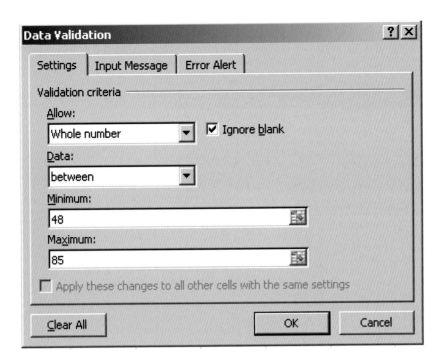

Figure 10.4

▶ Now we need to enter an **Input Message**. Click the **Input Message** tab and enter the text as shown in Figure 10.5.

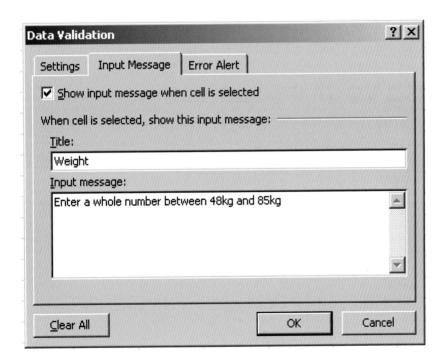

Figure 10.5

▶ Finally, we'll enter an **Error Alert** message. Select the **Error Alert** tab at the top of the dialogue box.

The message we enter here is the message that will appear if someone enters an invalid value.

Choose a **Style** from the left drop-down list. Type the message **Weight must be a whole number between 48kg and 85kg**. Give it the title **Weight**.

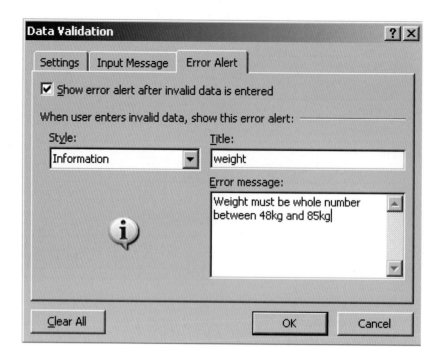

Figure 10.6

 Click **OK** to close the dialogue box.

Testing your validation

It is important to try and enter some invalid values into the cell to make sure that the validation rule works. You must make sure that it rejects invalid values but it is equally important to make sure that it accepts valid values – if not you'll have to go back and check the settings!

 Click in cell **C3**. You will see your **Input Message**. Try entering **45**. Press **Enter**.

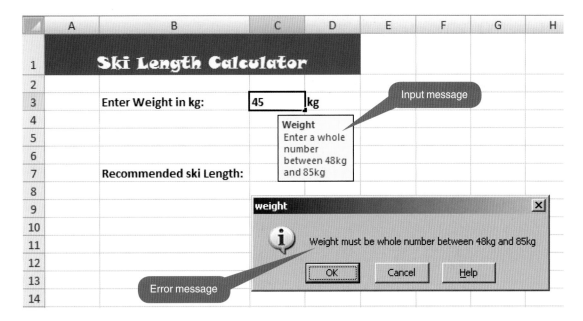

Figure 10.7

▶ Now enter **59**. The value should be accepted. Try a few more values to reassure yourself the validation rule is working correctly.

▶ Save your work.

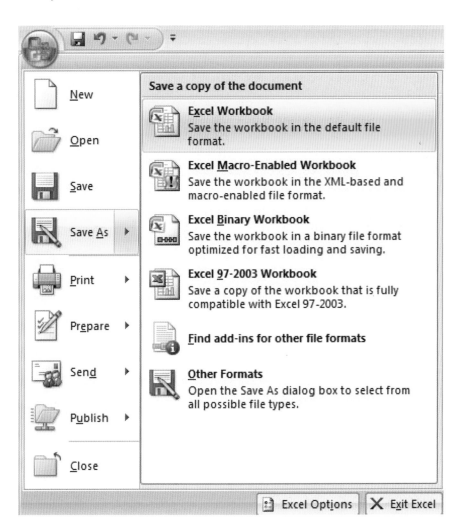

Figure 10.8

The VLOOKUP function

The VLOOKUP function is what we'll use to automatically display the correct ski length based on the weight entered.

 Select cell C7. Swap to the Formulas tab and click the down-arrow next to the AutoSum button in the Function library group (on the left-hand side of the Ribbon). Select More Functions ...

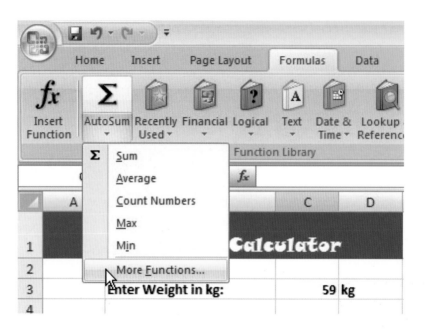

Figure 10.9

 The Insert Function dialogue box loads:

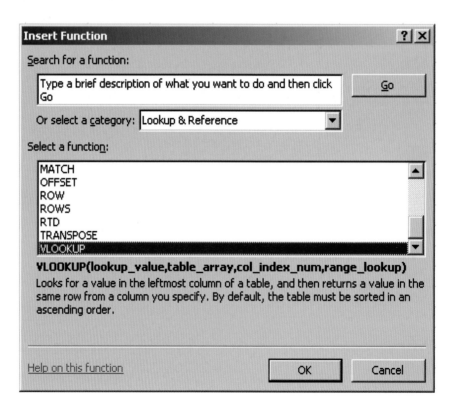

Figure 10.10

▶ Change to the **Lookup & Reference** selection in the 'Or select a category' box.

▶ Find **VLOOKUP** at the bottom of the function list. Click **OK**.

▶ The **Lookup_value** is the cell you want to find in a table. You need to **enter C3** here.

▶ Enter **SkiLength** in the **Table_array** box. This is the range that contains **all** of the lengths on the **SkiLengthChart** sheet.

VLOOKUP will look for the value you entered in cell **C3** in the left-most column **of** the range that you entered – that is the **Minimum Weight** column. If it can't find **the** exact value (for example, if you enter **65**) it will default to the nearest value **less than** **65** and find the ski length for someone whose minimum weight is **64**. For this **reason** VLOOKUP will not work unless the **Table_array** you refer to is sorted in **Ascending** order (which is the case following the original typing of the list, so you do not **need to** alter this).

▶ Now you need to find the ski length from the third column in the table, so enter **3** in the **Col_index_num** box.

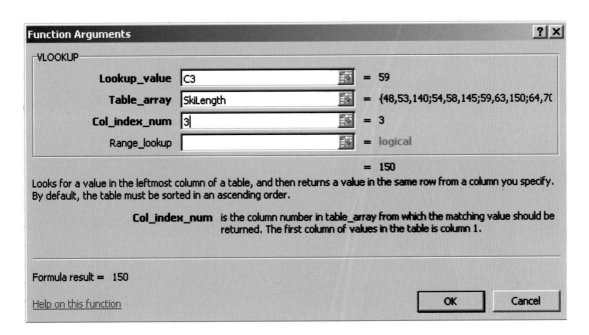

Figure 10.11

▶ Click **OK**.

▶ Try changing the customer weight in cell **C3**. **What happens?**

▶ Save the spreadsheet.

Chapter 11 – Macros and Buttons

In this chapter we'll add a new column to the ski length chart to include recommended ski lengths for intermediate level skiers. We'll then use macros and buttons on the main screen so that the user can specify whether the customer is a beginner or intermediate.

 Load Excel and open the **SkiCalculator** spreadsheet.

 Click on the **SkiLengthChart** sheet tab. Add a column of recommended ski lengths for intermediate level skiers as shown in Figure 11.1.

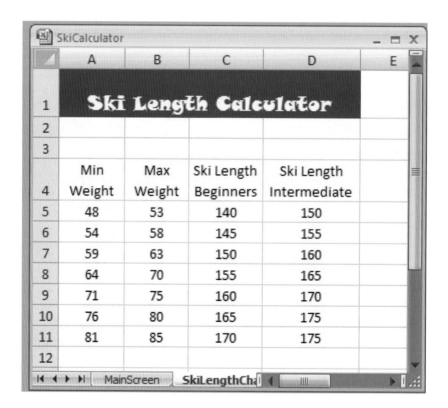

Figure 11.1

Redefining a named range

▶ Now that we've added another column, we need to redefine the **SkiLength** range that we named in the last chapter.

▶ Swap to the **Formulas** tab and click the **Name Manager** button.

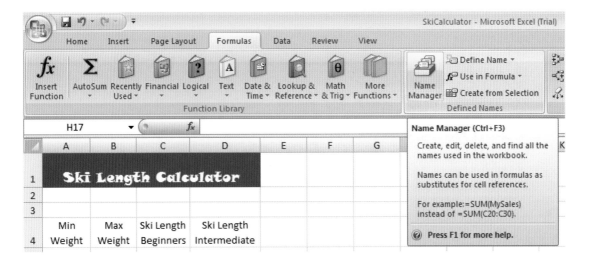

Figure 11.2

▶ Select **SkiLength**. In the **Refers to:** box, click the **Collapse Dialogue** button.

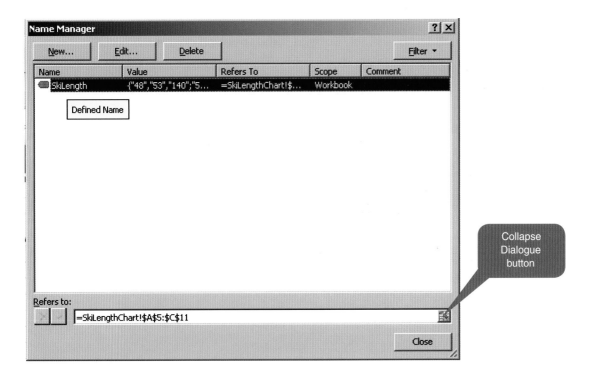

Figure 11.3

▷ Re-select a new range of cells to include the new column (**D5** to **D11**).

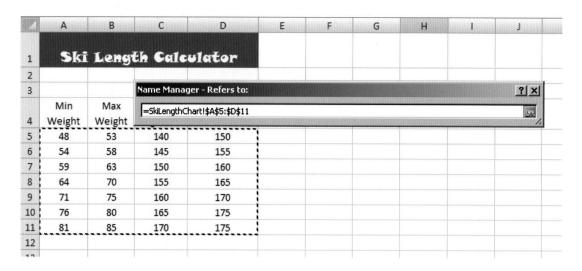

	A	B	C	D	E	F	G	H	I	J
1	Ski Length Calculator									
2										
3			Name Manager - Refers to:						?|x	
4	Min Weight	Max Weight	=SkiLengthChart!$A$5:$D$11							
5	48	53	140	150						
6	54	58	145	155						
7	59	63	150	160						
8	64	70	155	165						
9	71	75	160	170						
10	76	80	165	175						
11	81	85	170	175						
12										

Figure 11.4

▷ Press **Enter**. Click **Close** and then **Yes**.

The Format Painter button

▷ Return to the **MainScreen** sheet.

▷ In cell **B5** type **Enter Skier Ability Level:**.

▷ Select cell **B3** and click the **Format Painter** button on the **Home** tab.

Figure 11.5

▷ Now click in cell **B5**.

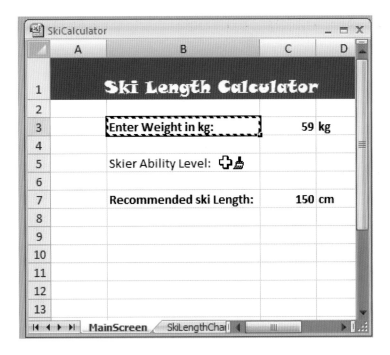

Figure 11.6

The formatting of cell **B3** will be copied to cell **B5**!

Selecting values from a drop-down list

In cell **C5** the user needs to specify either **Beginner** or **Intermediate**. It would be nice if the user could select an option from a list rather than typing it in. This will be quicker and will eliminate the chances of the user making a spelling error; the computer wouldn't be able to recognise a misspelt word and would return either an error message or a wrong value.

 Click in cell **F2** and type **Beginner**. Type **Intermediate** in cell **F3**.

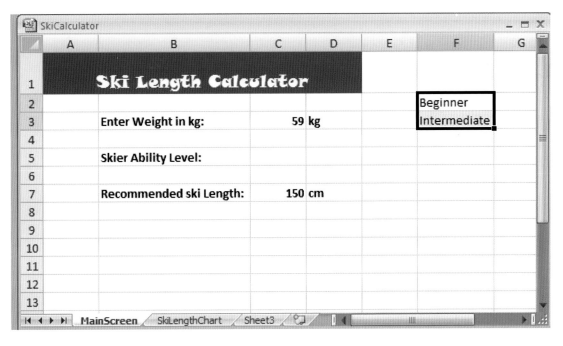

Figure 11.7

▶ Now click in cell **C5**. Swap to the **Data** tab and in the **Data Tools** group click the **Data Validation** button.

▶ Under the **Settings** tab, choose **List** from the **Allow:** menu.

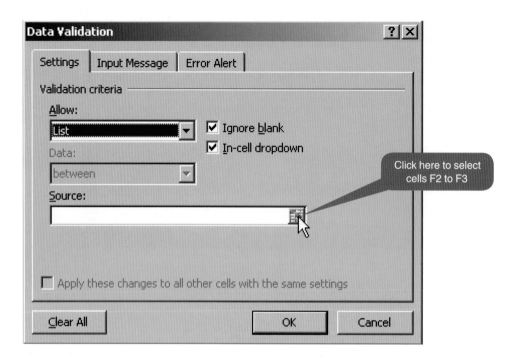

Figure 11.8

▶ Tab to the **Source:** box and on the spreadsheet, highlight cells **F2** to **F3**.

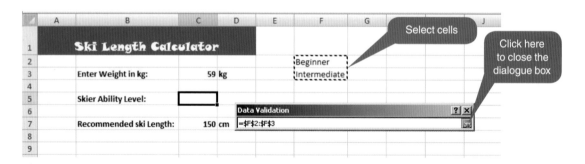

Figure 11.9

▶ Close the **Data Validation** selection box as shown in Figure 11.9.

▶ In the **Data Validation** dialogue box click **OK**.

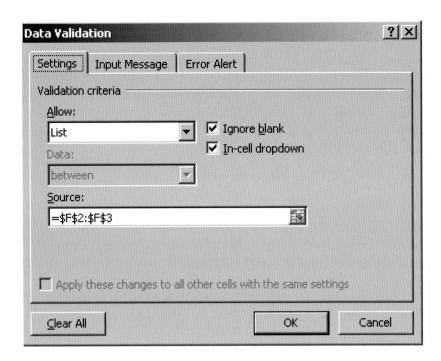

Figure 11.10

▶ Click on the small down-arrow next to cell **C5** and see what appears!

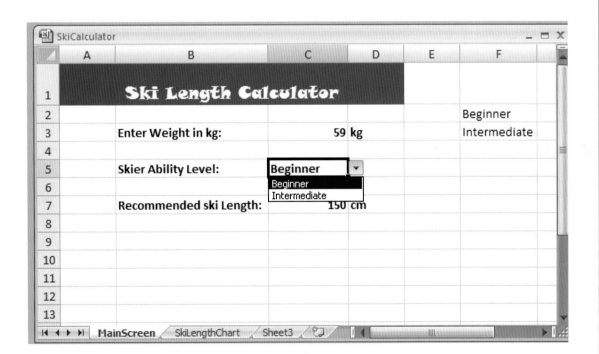

Figure 11.11

▶ You can colour the text in cells **F2** and **F3** white to hide it if you like.

IF ... THEN ... ELSE ... and VLOOKUP

Now we need to add an **IF** statement to cell **C7** so that Excel looks up different ski lengths for beginner and intermediate skiers; at the moment it is set up to give the ski lengths for beginners only.

The logic goes something like this:

IF **Beginner** is selected, THEN look up the ski length from the **Beginner** column, ELSE look up the ski length from the **Intermediate** column.

To do the looking up, we will need to use the **VLOOKUP** function again, so in fact we are using one function inside another. To start off with we will just do the IF ... THEN part. When that works we can add the ELSE ... part!

▶ Select cell **C7**. The formula needs to be amended.

▶ Click in the **Formula** bar to edit the formula.

▶ Position the cursor just after the = at the beginning of the formula.

▶ Type **IF(C5='Beginner'**, but **DO NOT** press **Enter** yet! You need to fill in the rest of the formula as shown in Figure 11.12.

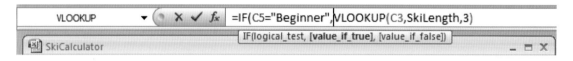

Figure 11.12

▶ At the end of the formula add a closing bracket). Press **Enter**.

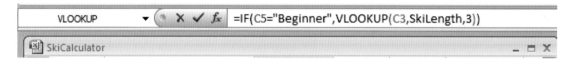

Figure 11.13

▶ Test the new formula by choosing **Beginner** as the ability level and changing the customer's weight.

It should work! Now you can add the last part of the formula to tell Excel what to do if **Intermediate** is selected as the ability level.

▶ Click in cell **C7** and delete the last closing bracket). Type in a comma , instead.

Now add another **VLOOKUP** formula to find the ski length for **Intermediate** skiers.

▶ Type in **VLOOKUP(C3, SkiLength,** but **DO NOT** press **Enter**!

This time you will need to look in the fourth column of the **SkiLength** table, so the last part of the **VLOOKUP** formula will be a **4** instead of a **3**.

▶ Enter a **4** and two closing brackets)): one for the **VLOOKUP** function and one for the **IF** statement.

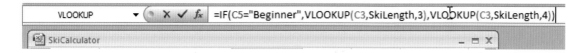

Figure 11.14

▶ Make sure you've entered the formula correctly, then press **Enter**.

Test your new system!

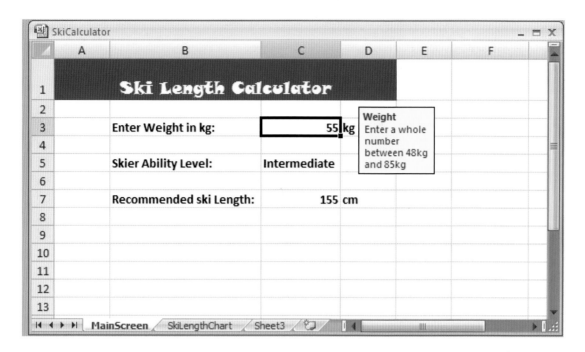

Figure 11.15

▶ Save your work.

Creating a menu screen

We need to create another new sheet which will display a brief menu of options. A menu screen would be more important if you had included a more comprehensive table of winter sports information, such as a table of snowboard sizes. As it is, the menu screen will give the user a choice of calculating the ski length or viewing the ski length chart.

▶ Click the **Insert Worksheet** button.

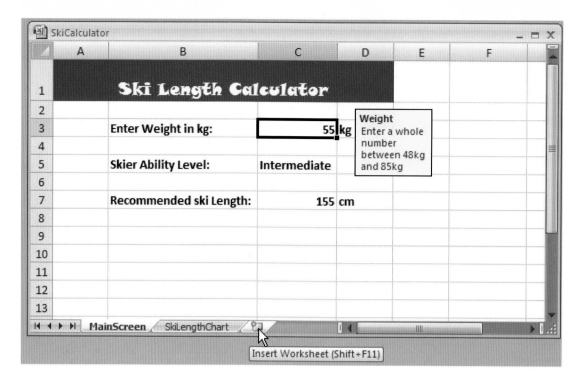

Figure 11.16

▶ Right click the new tab and select **Rename**. Type in **Menu** and press **Enter**.

▶ Right click the tab again and select **Tab Colour ...**

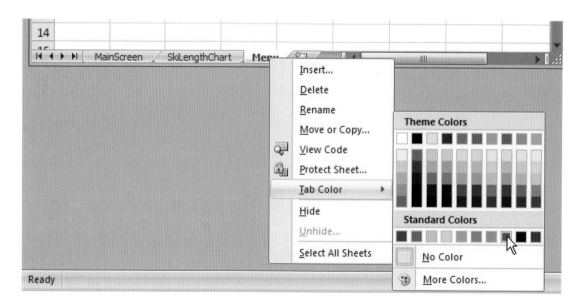

Figure 11.17

▶ Change the colour to blue. Click **OK**.

▶ Design a menu screen like the one shown in Figure 11.18.

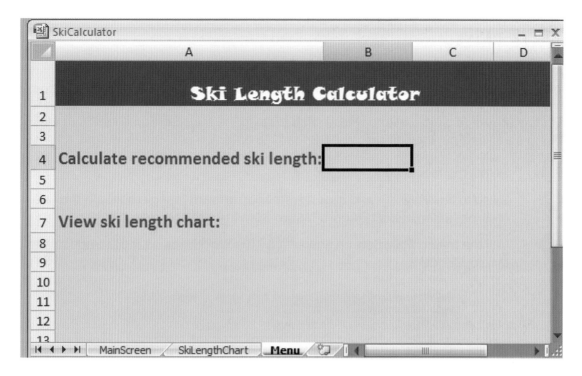

Figure 11.18

Adding clip art

▷ Select the **Insert** tab and click the **Clip Art** button.

▷ Select a suitable picture and move it into position on your menu screen.

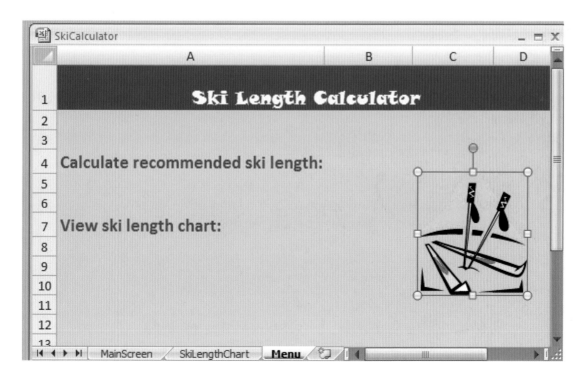

Figure 11.19

▷ Save your work.

Macros

A macro is a series of commands that is stored and grouped to run as a single command when you activate it by using a particular keystroke combination or by pressing a button.

For this project, a simple macro will be used to go to the **MainScreen** sheet from the **Menu** sheet and put the cursor in cell **C3** ready to enter the customer's weight.

▶ Select the **Menu** worksheet.

▶ Swap to the **View** tab and click the small downward triangle beneath the **Macros** button. Select **Record Macro** from the shortcut menu.

▶ Call the macro **MainScreen** and select **This Workbook** as the storage for the macro. Click **OK**.

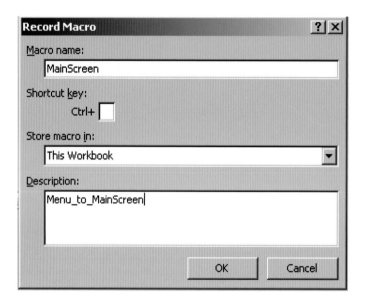

Figure 11.20

You are now in recording mode. Everything you do now will be recorded by Excel. Be careful here!

▶ Click on the **MainScreen** tab.

▶ Click in cell **C3**.

▶ Click the **Stop Recording** button (click the small downward triangle beneath the **Macros** button to reveal the button). All done!

Figure 11.21

Buttons

Now you need to add a button which will run the macro. The tool for doing this is not normally found on the **Ribbon**, so the first task is to place the **Button** tool on the **Quick Access Toolbar**, which is a bit of a rigmarole really, but necessary!

 Click the **Office** button and then the **Excel Options** button at the bottom of the shortcut menu.

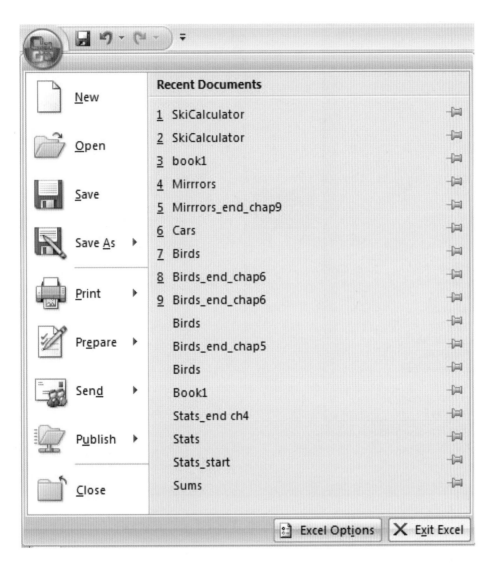

Figure 11.22

In the **Excel Options** dialogue box select **Customize** and in the **Choose commands from** drop-down box, select **Commands Not in the Ribbon**.

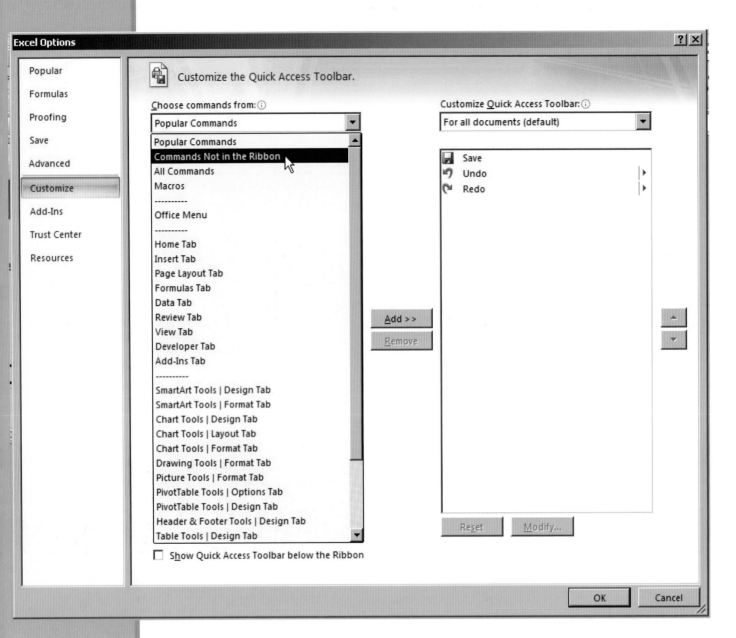

Figure 11.23

 Select the **Button (Form Control)** tool and click the central **Add** button. This places the **Button** tool on the **Quick Access Toolbar**. Click **OK**.

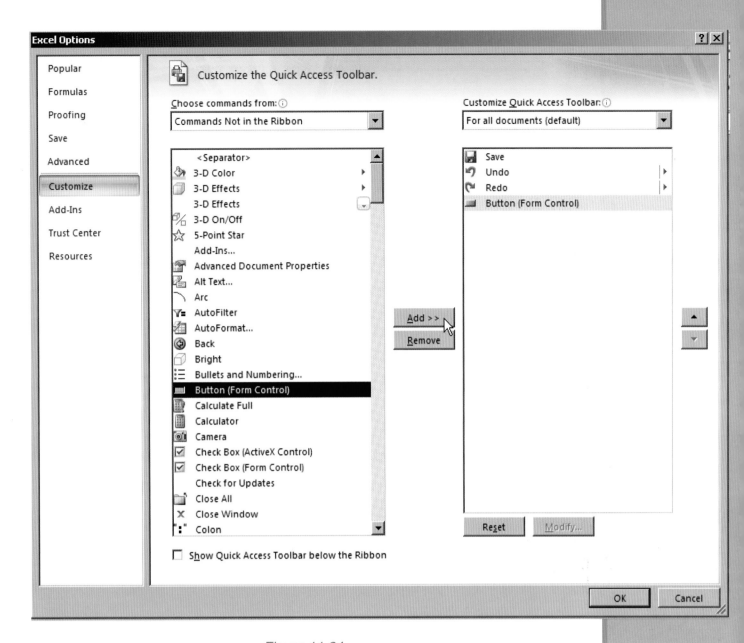

Figure 11.24

▶ Figure 11.25 shows the new control added to the **Quick Access Toolbar**. The rest, thankfully, is quite straightforward.

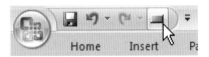

Figure 11.25

▶ Click the **Button** tool and draw, using the cross-hairs, a suitably positioned and sized button on the **Menu** sheet; you may need to move or resize the **ClipArt** graphic to give sufficient room for the button.

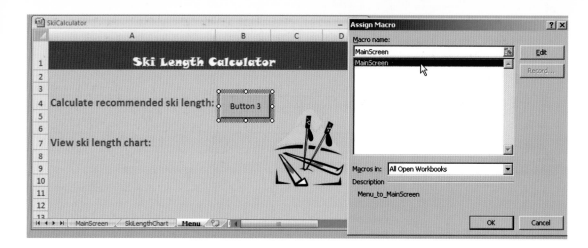

Figure 11.26

▶ When you have finished drawing the button, the **Assign Macro** dialogue box appears; you can now link the button to the macro. Click the macro name to link the macro to your button (see Figure 11.26) and then click **OK**.

▶ To change the caption on the button, highlight the current text (which is probably **Button 1**) and type in your new caption. You can easily change the caption's font size etc. by right clicking on the button and selecting the **Format Control** option from the shortcut menu.

▶ Check that it works.

▶ Now use the same method to create another macro and second button to enable the user to go to the ski length chart.

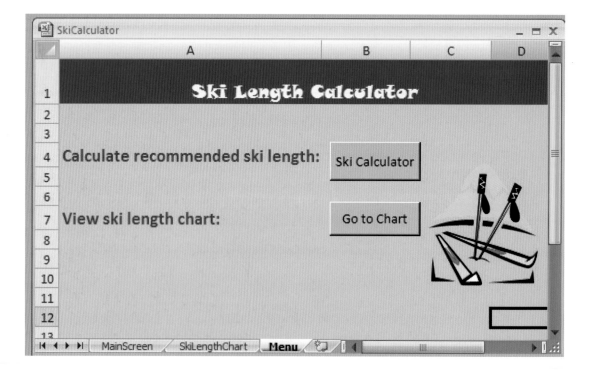

Figure 11.27

▶ You could extend the project and make macros and their associated buttons to return from the **SkiLengthChart** and **MainScreen** sheets to the **Menu** sheet.

Finally, when you save your work, you will have to save the spreadsheet as a **Macro-Enabled Workbook** and enable macros (**Office Button > Excel Options > Trust Center > Trust Center Settings > Enable all Macros**) if you intend to rerun this project.

That's it! Save your work and go book a holiday!

Index